"Well researched with careful detail; beautifully and thoughtfully written."

—Carol Carter, actor and playwright

"*Pauli Murray's Revolutionary Life* is a fascinating untold story of apartheid America of the last century recounted in a straightforward, heartfelt manner that will have you both leaping for joy over Pauli's successes and in tears over the humiliations she refused to suffer gracefully as a queer woman of color."

—Dennis Broe, journalism professor and author of *A Hello to Arms*

"Black civil rights activist and pioneering feminist Pauli Murray's unique story reaches a new audience with this lively narrative about her trailblazing life and her very American roots that crossed the color line. We see how she rode freight trains during the Great Depression, planned lunch counter sit-ins in the 1940s, and challenged the boundaries of gender identity, as she became one of the first women ordained in the Episcopal Church."

—Bill Fletcher Jr., labor activist and author of *The Man Who Fell from the Sky*

"*Pauli Murray's Revolutionary Life* is an intriguing primer not just about a potent political activist's lifelong adventures. The author's easy storytelling provides readers with an intimate tour—via this fascinating woman's daring experiences—of America's racist history and its heroic 20th century struggles for civil rights."

—Peter Laufer, University of Oregon journalism professor and author of *Up Against the Wall: The Case for Opening the Mexican-American Border*

Pauli Murray's Revolutionary Life

Pauli Murray's Revolutionary Life

Simki Kuznick

Rootstock Publishing
Montpelier, VT

First Printing: March 2022

Pauli Murray's Revolutionary Life, Copyright © 2022 by Simki Kuznick

Release Date: March 1, 2022

Hardcover ISBN: 978-1-57869-077-0
Softcover ISBN: 978-1-57869-076-3
eBook ISBN: 978-1-57869-078-7

Library of Congress Control Number: 2021917275

Published by Rootstock Publishing
an imprint of Multicultural Media, Inc.
27 Main Street, Suite 6
Montpelier, VT 05602 USA

www.rootstockpublishing.com

info@rootstockpublishing.com

Interior and cover design by Eddie Vincent, ENC Graphic Services (ed.vincent@encirclepub.com)

Cover art: Cover photograph courtesy of FDR Presidential Library & Museum. Dr. Murray sent this photo to Eleanor Roosevelt in December 1955.

Author photo credit: Larry Levner

For permissions or to schedule an author interview, contact the author at simki.kuznick@aol.com.

Printed in the USA

Author's Note

Source material is primarily from Pauli Murray's two memoirs and published poetry: *Proud Shoes: The Story of An American Family* (Harper and Row, New York, 1956, 1978, 1984); *Song in a Weary Throat: An American Pilgrimage* (Harper and Row, New York, 1987); and *Dark Testament and other poems* (Silvermine Publishers, Norwalk, Conn., 1970). Some dialogue is taken directly from Murray's personal observations. As scholars increased the knowledge of Murray's life through private papers archived at the Schlesinger Library, Radcliffe Institute, Harvard University, further material is from the following books: *The Firebrand and the First Lady, Portrait of a Friendship* by Patricia Bell-Scott (Alfred A. Knopf, New York, 2016); *Jane Crow: The Life of Pauli Murray* by Rosalind Rosenberg (Oxford University Press, New York, 2017); and *Pauli Murray, A Personal and Political Life* by Troy R. Saxby (University of North Carolina Press, Chapel Hill, 2020).

Contents

Dedication

To my daughters Asmara Beraki Marek and Sara Ghebremichael and to the memory of Barthélémy Roussève who first introduced me to Pauli Murray's story.

Introduction

People often ask me how I knew about Pauli Murray since she is only recently getting the recognition she deserves. In 1972, when I went on a student trip to Ghana, where Murray spent a year teaching constitutional law, I became friends with the coordinator Barthélémy Rousseve. He was from New Orleans with Creole heritage. Around 1985, the year Murray passed away, Bart gave me a book called *Proud Shoes* about Murray's ancestors because of my interest in interracial families—I was married to an Eritrean-American immigrant. With our two daughters, we had joined an organization called Interracial Pride in Berkeley, California, to share our joys and concerns with families like our own.

I learned more about Pauli's amazing life in 1987, when I read her posthumous memoir, *Song in A Weary Throat*. I thought the stories of Pauli's fearless adventures riding freight trains, hitchhiking with her girlfriends, striving to be at the top of her class, and resisting segregation's ridiculous restrictions, would be an inspiring story for young people. I wanted to combine it with her family's very American interracial history, starting with her White great-grandmother in Delaware who married a free Black man who later fought in the Civil War. And moving to her grandmother whose Cherokee mother was raped by her White father, the son of a North Carolina planter who had been a Congressman during President Monroe's term.

I tried to find a publisher after Barack Obama's historic election, but I heard the same refrain, "Wow, what an interesting woman, but she isn't well known enough to sell a book about her life." Meanwhile scholars were researching Murray's papers and discovering her complicated personal life. They explored her love affairs with women and her feeling that she was more male than female, and I wrote this aspect of her life into this book. Pauli's recognition grew. In 2016, her family home in Durham, North Carolina was designated a National Historic Landmark, sponsored by the Pauli Murray Center. In 2017, Yale University, where she had received her second law degree, named a new college after her. And, in 2021, a documentary called "My Name is Pauli Murray," produced by the directors of "RBG," was released.

As a new generation is becoming aware of the roots of systemic racism propelled by the Black Lives Matter movement, people are learning how influential and ahead of her time Pauli Murray was in the pursuit of civil rights. She was arrested in Virginia for not moving to the back of the bus in 1940, and organized cafeteria sit-ins in Washington, DC, in 1943. Her 1944 Howard law school paper arguing that separate could never be equal was used to prepare the case for Brown v. Board of Education ten years later.

People are also discovering that Pauli Murray was one of the founders of the National Organization for Women (NOW), which is still fighting today against new laws like the Texas Heartbeat Act that seeks to overturn the 48-year-old precedent of Roe v. Wade. Pauli helped write NOW's original mission statement in 1966, making sure that equity was addressed: "We realize that women's problems are linked to many broader questions of social justice." She coined the phrase "Jane Crow," and her ideas contributed to Ruth Bader Ginsburg's argument that the 14th Amendment also applied to discrimination against women. Her personal life speaks to our acknowledgement of gender fluidity. As one of the first female Episcopal priests, she lectured that her "entire life's quest has been for spiritual integration, where there is no East or West, no Black or White, no Male or Female."

Pauli Murray knew that she was ahead of her time. She kept some of her life hidden so that she could carry on her work for social justice and equality. Now we can celebrate the fullness of her life. Now her story can inspire a new generation to fight the hard fight for an integrated, just, and equitable world for all living beings to live in harmony on this beautiful earth.

—Simki Ghebremichael Kuznick
March 2022

Chapter 1

Past Associations

Pauli bounded up the steps of the Brooklyn Avenue subway. At forty-two, she had the lean frame and nervous energy of a twenty-year-old. Her short-cropped curly hair revealed she was a woman who didn't waste time on appearances. She put her hands in the pockets of her wool coat to warm them against the winter chill as she walked the few blocks to her apartment, which she shared with her two aunts.

After taking the steps two at a time to the third floor, Pauli was greeted by her Shetland sheepdog, Smokey, who sat by the door anticipating her return. She knelt down to give his head and ears a good rub. After she hung her coat on a peg in the hall, she saw the letter from Cornell University on the mahogany side table. She brought the envelope into the kitchen where Aunt Sallie and Aunt Pauline were setting out the evening meal. The two elderly women had come to live with Pauli after they retired from teaching in Durham, North Carolina.

"It's from the dean of the college," Pauli said as she sat down at the table crowded with a plate of warm buttermilk biscuits, bowls of steaming vegetables, and a hearty platter of meatloaf. Smokey lay down patiently on his rug in the corner.

Pauli had applied for a job at Cornell University as a research assistant to the director of codification of the laws of Liberia, a country in West Africa settled in 1822 by Africans freed from bondage in America. After World War II, countries in Africa were just beginning to achieve independence after centuries of being ruled by colonial European powers. Pauli wanted to be part of the liberation of these countries. She also wanted to apply for this position because so few people of color were representing America overseas in 1952. She was troubled that after supplying her usual references, the school had asked her to submit further documentation of her background.

In her work as a lawyer, Pauli was used to stringent background checks. Before being admitted to the California State Bar in 1945, she had to provide an affidavit attesting to her integrity. Later, when she applied to the New York State Bar, the Committee on Character and Fitness asked her to fill out an extensive form to verify her loyalty to the United States. To apply for the job at Cornell, Pauli had submitted personal references from many respected officials: former First Lady Eleanor Roosevelt, whom she had gotten to know during the Great Depression after sending her a letter protesting inhumane treatment at the welfare office; Judge William H. Hastie, her professor at Howard Law School who sat on the bench of the US Court of Appeals; labor leader A. Philip Randolph, head of the Brotherhood of Sleeping Car Porters, a national railroad workers' union; Lloyd K. Garrison, descendent of White abolitionist William Lloyd Garrison; and future Supreme Court Justice Thurgood Marshall.

But the political climate had changed in the United States after WWII. Tensions were rising between the US and the Soviet Union, a Communist country that had been America's ally during the war when the US was fighting against Nazi Germany. Concern that communist ideas might spread to America was causing fear and mistrust. Something in Pauli's background made the university hesitant to offer her the job.

Pauli knew that no job was ever guaranteed, not for an African

American woman, no matter how brilliant or high achieving she was. But she always stubbornly tried to overcome whatever obstacles stood in her way. She had achieved many firsts. When she'd enrolled in Richmond High School in Queens, New York, to prepare for her entrance into Hunter College, she was the only African American among four thousand students. At Hunter, where there were only one hundred women of color out of five thousand, she was one of only four who graduated in a class of 247. At Howard University, a historically Black college founded in 1867, she was one of the few women to graduate from the School of Law. She was the first female elected president of her class and the first woman to be elected Chief Justice of the Court of Peers by the Howard Law Student Guild.

Pauli read through the letter in silence while her aunts anxiously awaited the news.

"Tell us, dear," urged her namesake, Aunt Pauline, who had raised Pauli since she was four.

"Don't keep us in suspense," Aunt Sallie added. "At our age, our hearts can't take it." But, having endured a long life of disappointments, the two women already knew something was wrong.

Pauli tried to keep her composure as she told her aunts what the letter said. "It seems there are some questions concerning my 'past associations,' which might place the university in a difficult situation. They say there is 'no question in their minds as to my high character, integrity, and personal honesty, or my qualifications for the job,' but because of the 'troublesome times in which we live,'" she read aloud, "they need to have 'one hundred percent protection' regarding 'public relations.'"

Pauli stood up from the table and dropped the letter on the floor in disgust. Smokey followed her as she paced the confines of their small kitchen.

"They aren't even saying why I am being rejected. Their words are so vague. They haven't mentioned anything specific about my behavior that I could even dispute. They talk about my 'past associations,' as if there is some disgrace in knowing these people in the highest levels of government who spoke for me. They ask about my relationship to my country, but just leave the question hanging, without giving me a chance to clear my name!"

Her aunts watched in sympathetic silence while Pauli patted Smokey's head distractedly as he nuzzled his head into her knees. "After all my years of struggle to prepare myself, how can I be chopped down now at the very moment I reach for my greatest opportunity? First I am discriminated against because of my color, then my sex, and now the fear and suspicion that is overtaking our land strips me of my individuality and discards me like unwanted refuse." Pauli sat down almost near tears, but after a life of struggle, she seldom allowed herself to cry.

"You're going too far now, Pauli," warned Aunt Pauline. "This is just one more test of your character that you will overcome. You have only to trust in the Lord and not lose faith in yourself. Trust that He has a plan for you."

"Sometimes," offered Aunt Sallie, "when one door in life is closed against us, God opens up another door to a greater opportunity than we ourselves could have planned."

Aunt Pauline added sternly, "Remember that you come from a long line of proud Americans. Your ancestors instilled in you a deep pride in your American heritage and the strength and determination to rebel against injustice."

"Our people held our ground and refused to be cowed by adversity," Aunt Sallie echoed.

"Grandfather Fitzgerald fought for the Union in the Civil War," Pauli continued. "How can they doubt our patriotism? Because of Grandfather, we felt we belonged, that we had a stake in our country's future. We clung to that notion no matter how often it was snatched away from us."

"And don't forget your Smith heritage," Aunt Sallie chimed in playfully. "Grandmother Cornelia Smith wouldn't let you forget

Pauli's maternal grandparents, Robert and Cornelia Smith Fitzgerald of Durham NC, 1910.

them. We are descendants of the Smiths who helped found the University of North Carolina at Chapel Hill in 1792. And of Dr. James Smith who was a congressman during President Monroe's term."

"Now don't be bringing up Grandmother's father, that scallywag lawyer, Sidney Smith. He's nothin' we're proud of," Aunt Pauline reminded them.

Pauli veered away from that sore subject. "And what about Great-Grandfather Thomas Fitzgerald, a free man of color before Emancipation, who helped lay the bricks for Ashmun Institute, the first college for Colored men in Pennsylvania? It's called Lincoln University now."

"Yes," continued Aunt Pauline, "and your great-grandmother Sarah Ann, the daughter of White settlers in Delaware. She worked so hard to bring the family through difficult times."

Pauli sighed and looked at her two dear aunts, whom she loved so much. She felt a pressing need to learn everything she could about her deep American roots and to tell of her family's heroic struggle to find a secure place in American society.

"Aunt Pauline and Aunt Sallie, I've been wanting to tell our story, and this rejection on these flimsy grounds gives me the fighting spirit to do it!"

That very evening Pauli started writing down her recollections. She vowed to interview all members of her family to get at the real story. Her research would take her to the National Archives in Washington, DC, to search through census records, and the Chester

County Courthouse in Pennsylvania to find the deed to her great-grandfather's farm. Her stolid aunts sometimes stood right over her shoulder as she was typing on her beloved old Corona, each telling her own version of their family stories, as Pauli tried to sort it all out.

Fitzgerald family portrait. Left to right, back row: Mary Pauline, Agnes, and Sallie. First row: Cornelia, Robert, and Roberta.

Chapter 2

Pauli's Parents

Pauli's mother, Agnes, wanted to be a nurse, but in the early part of the twentieth century nursing wasn't considered a proper profession for a young woman from an educated African American family. Who knew what unwanted intimacies she would be exposed to, not to mention the risk of disease? Agnes was a sickly child. Her mother, Cornelia, would say, "Seems like every little infection that comes through town decides to take lodging in that girl's tiny frame." But Agnes always pulled her weight, what little there was of it, helping out on the farm with her brother and four sisters. She could ride a horse, pitch a bale of hay, drive a truck to market, cook up supper for her hungry family, and sew a fine dress if she needed to.

After she finished high school, Agnes traveled up from Durham to visit her older sister, Pauline, in Hampton, Virginia. Pauline had a position teaching elementary school. She had recently married a bright young lawyer, Charles Dame, who was a graduate of Howard Law School in Washington, DC. When Agnes decided to enroll in the Hampton Training School for Nurses, Pauline helped persuade their parents to let her go, even though they worried that being a nurse could expose Agnes to life-threatening illnesses.

Agnes met her future husband, William Murray, at Hampton Institute when he was enrolled in the Hampton Teacher Training Program. Mr. Murray, as they always called him, took Agnes's cousin Sadie to a dance at Buckroe Beach. Away from the supervision of their parents, Agnes and her sister Sallie decided to go to the dance by themselves without waiting for a man to ask them. Their sister, Marie, sewed Agnes a frilly dress made of pink dotted Swiss fabric. Marie was a professional dressmaker who sewed for many of the White society ladies in Hampton.

Mr. Murray kept his eye on Agnes all through the evening. He took care to notice when she and her sister were leaving, and he hustled their cousin Sadie onto the same streetcar, guiding Sadie toward the two sisters without her realizing it. After they formally met, Sadie teased him. "Why did you wait this long to ask for introductions? Agnes was at the dance all this time."

Will blushed and said, "I thought it would seem frivolous for the president of the campus YMCA to be so forward."

When Agnes returned home she realized, to her embarrassment, that she was wearing her pretty pink dress inside out!

"Oh, Sallie, how will I live this down?" she asked.

But Will didn't seem to notice. He wrote a formal letter to Pauline asking if he could start seeing Agnes. Mr. Murray went back to Baltimore for a time, and he and Agnes wrote letters to each other every week. They became engaged and planned to be married after Agnes graduated from nursing school.

The wedding took place in Durham, and Marie was again pressed into service, this time to fashion a bridal gown for her sister. Marie's young husband had recently passed away from tuberculosis, or "galloping consumption" as they called it then. Marie had come home to have their baby, but the wedding was so close to the baby's arrival date, Marie couldn't attend the ceremony. "You won't be going to the church and start having your pains when they're saying their vows!" Cornelia scolded.

Marie helped Agnes with her dress while the others went on to the church. She couldn't help but take her time putting in a tuck at the waistline and straightening the hem to make the bride look her best while the groom and all the guests were fanning themselves in the heat of Emmanuel Church, wondering what was taking the bride so long!

"Come now, Marie," Agnes fretted. "Are you finished fussing with me yet? Mr. Murray is waiting for me at the church."

"Don't you just look pretty as a picture, Agnes?" Marie gushed, surveying her artistry. "Why, I've never seen such a beautiful bride, if I do say so myself," she said as she giggled. "Turn around. Let me see you from all sides."

As they stood in front of the mirror, they could hear the faint murmur of thunder a few miles away. Their brother, Charles, who had been pacing outside next to the hired horse and buggy that would take them to church, called impatiently from the front hall. "Agnes, you better get a move on if we're gonna make it to the church before that storm hits."

"I think we're finally ready, Charles," Agnes called back. "We'll be down right soon."

Agnes looked at her dress one more time in the mirror, with Marie standing proudly behind her. Then Agnes saw the strained expression that tightened Marie's face. Marie made a sharp cry and doubled over, her two hands covering her round, extended stomach.

"Oh, Agnes," she gasped, trying to catch her breath. "I think it might be time. What should we do? I can't spoil your wedding."

Marie stood petrified, staring at Agnes while Agnes sized up the situation using her skills as a nurse.

"You'll set down on that bed right now and wait till I get this dress off so I can help you." But first she called downstairs to her brother.

"Charles! Charles, go run and tell the doctor to come right away. Marie's starting her labor. You go and get him and bring him back here in the buggy. And then you go on to the church and tell the folks that Marie is having her time. Tell Mr. Murray I can't come to the church right now. Our wedding will have to wait."

It was a difficult birth. The thunder and lightening of the storm only added to the tension, but Agnes remained calm throughout and helped bring little Jeffrey into the world on July 1, 1903. In the afternoon, she put her wedding dress back on, headed to Emmanuel Church, and married William Murray.

Pauli's parents,
William Henry Murray, 1872-1923, and
Agnes Fitzgerald Murray, 1878-1914.

Like so many young people of his day, William became a schoolteacher because he wanted to provide children with the tools to find opportunities for a better life, which had been denied to his people for so long. He was following in the footsteps of his father-in-law, Robert Fitzgerald, who had come to Durham from Pennsylvania to start a school for newly emancipated children. Will always said, "I am a teacher because I believe it is so important to instill pride in the Colored boys and girls who are facing a world that only seeks to keep them down."

But he was a man of many talents. In college he was captain of a semiprofessional baseball team. He knew all the marches of John Philip Sousa on the piano and played flute in a local band. He loved hunting and fishing. He even raised carrier pigeons, for a time, in his backyard.

Agnes and Will already had three children when he came down with typhoid fever, a few years before Pauli was born. In the sweltering heat of the summer, Agnes used all her nursing skills as she fought to keep him alive.

Agnes wrote her sister Pauline:

> *Neither money nor labor has been spared in treating Will's case. It has been the finest and best that money could secure. Everything one could get in the best hospitals. I know I have made a city-wide reputation for myself among both White and Black, for everyone seems anxious and worried about Will. The fine White physicians are delighted with my efficiency in nursing him—'for a Colored,' they add. They said I must have had great experience in nursing typhoid fever. Oh, Pauline, I would rather die with my Will than live without him.*

Will pulled through, but as a result of the illness he began to have attacks of depression, and his moods became violent and unpredictable. To find some relief from Will's erratic behavior, Agnes occasionally took her son, Willie, her daughters Grace and Mildred, and her youngest child, named after her sister Pauline, to visit her family in Durham. Her sister Pauline's marriage had broken up and she had returned to Durham to live in the house at the bottom of Maplewood Cemetery with her parents and their sister Sallie. Agnes would fill up a basket with enough fried chicken, hard-boiled eggs, and fresh lemonade in Mason jars to last them the whole train ride to North Carolina.

"Mama, why do we have to take our own food on the train?" Willie asked. "Uncle Joe who works on the trains says they have dining cars where they serve meals to the passengers."

"Colored folks aren't served food in the dining car," Agnes answered matter-of-factly. "Besides, I wouldn't trust the food they might serve to our people."

"Mama's food is better anyway," shrugged Grace.

Pauli was two years old the summer Agnes discovered she was pregnant again. With a heavy heart from all the trouble that lay ahead of her, Agnes was getting ready to board the train to take all the children back to Baltimore when her sister Pauline held firmly onto little Pauli's shoulders.

"Agnes," she said, "you have four little ones and one more on the way. That's too much for any woman to cope with alone. And Mr. Murray, with his condition . . ." She held Pauli so tightly against her breast, it nearly took the child's breath away. She said very firmly to Agnes, "I'm keeping Pauli with me until after your baby is born."

"But I can't leave my precious Pauli," Agnes agonized.

"Yes you can, Agnes. You don't need a baby in diapers to worry about right now."

"But her clothes are in the luggage on the train!" Agnes wailed.

"Don't worry about that. I'll find her something to wear. Mrs. Jones has a girl a little older than Pauli. She'll have some out-growns to give me."

Pauli ended up staying with Aunt Pauline for nine months. Agnes must have realized she needed the help. After a time she wrote her sister:

> *Is little Pauline still using her diapers? I do hope you will train her to use the chamber pot, for all these children require so much to be done for them, and I am not so strong.*

And later:

> *I believe it would lift Will's spirits if you could appear on the scene and have an old chat with him.*

By the time Pauline brought Pauli back to Baltimore, she was like a mother to little Pauli. When Agnes first reached out to hug her daughter, Pauli tried to hide in Aunt Pauline's skirts. Pauli's sisters and brother tried their best to include her. Grace and Mildred let Pauli play with their dolls. Willie tried to engage her in a game of catch, rolling a ball on the floor toward her. And her father took her on his knees and sang her a funny song. Her mother just hugged her and told her how much she loved her. "I'm so glad to have you home, sweetheart."

But Agnes took her sister aside and said something all too prescient. "If anything happens to me, I want you to have little Pauline. She is not like the other children and I'm afraid they will ruin her disposition."

"What on earth are you talking about?" Pauline shrugged. "I was only helping you out. Everything is going to be fine now."

"No, I mean it. I haven't been as well as I should be since the last baby. Please."

"All right, then. I'll remember."

Rosetta was a sickly toddler and the baby, Robert Fitzgerald, who was named after Pauli's grandfather, was still at Johns Hopkins Hospital because he was too frail to be brought home. He stayed at the hospital for six months.

When Pauli was four years old, she came down with the chicken pox. She was quarantined in a separate room on the third floor so she wouldn't expose the other children. She felt sad but somehow important to have this condition that required her to be away from the rest of the family. She made up games, counting the patterns on the wallpaper and making maps of Bible stories out of the cracks in the ceiling. She liked the mornings when she could hear the hustle and bustle of family life as Father helped get the children off to school. Then she felt sad when the house grew quiet except for baby Rosetta's cries.

On the third morning she got out of bed as usual and sat on the old trunk by the window so she could look down at the street below. She knew if she stretched her neck, she could just see Father, Grace, and Willie starting down the sidewalk. She heard Father calling from the front hall, "Willie, get some fire in your legs or we're going to be late."

"You've got to finish your porridge first, young man," Agnes scolded him in the kitchen.

"All right, Mother," Willie answered and called out, a last mouthful of oatmeal obscuring his words, "I'm coming, Father."

Pauli imagined Willie gulping a last swig of milk and gathering up his books, then kissing Mother goodbye. Pauli heard the door slam and then her mother's footsteps on the stairs. Pauli hoped her mother was coming up to see her and bring her breakfast, but she knew she had to wait until Mother finished feeding baby Rosetta before she'd have a moment to bring Pauli her breakfast. Suddenly, Pauli heard a great clatter on the stairs and heard her mother cry out. Out the window, she had just seen Grace walking primly ahead, but she hadn't seen Father yet. He must have heard Mother's fall from the front yard. Pauli heard his steps on the porch as he rushed back in the house, calling, "Agnes, Agnes, don't be sick now. Agnes, darling, we need you!"

Pauli stayed in her room because she had been told not to come out under any circumstances. They'd even put a chamber pot in there for her needs. Pauli sat on that trunk for a long time, banging her heels against the side. It took many minutes for anyone to remember her. She was hungry and upset when Grace finally came upstairs.

"Pauli, Mother is very sick again. You just stay up here till things get settled."

"But I'm hungry. I haven't had my porridge yet," Pauli pleaded.

"Just sit tight a little longer. I'll try to bring you up something to eat."

Pauli folded her arms resolutely against her chest and announced, "You just wait till my Aunt Pauline comes. She'll straighten things out." She didn't know yet that her mother had a blood clot in her brain. Agnes didn't make it to the hospital.

Aunt Pauline came on the very next train north. First she went straight to Johns Hopkins Hospital and brought little Robert Fitzgerald home. All of the children had to be split up. There were too many for Will to take care of alone. The older ones—Grace, Willie, and Mildred—would stay with Will. The younger ones would go with Will's sister and brother, Aunt Rose and Uncle Lewis, who were both unmarried and lived a few blocks away. But when Aunt Rose was putting the two babies into the baby carriage to take them home with her, Aunt Pauline took Pauli aside. She knelt down so she would be the same height as the little girl.

"Pauli, you can make up your mind to do whatever you want. I'm going to ask you what you want to do." She looked Pauli straight in the eye. "Do you want to go with Aunt Ruth and be with Rosetta and Robert Fitzgerald? You'll have Grace and Willie and Mildred and Father nearby. Or do you want to come back down to Durham, all the way on the train, to live with me and Aunt Sallie and your Grandfather Fitzgerald and Grandma Cornelia?" Pauli's hand was resting on the edge of the carriage and Rosetta had put her little fist around two of her fingers. Pauli looked hard at both of the babies and at Aunt Rose.

Pauline prodded her gently. "Child, it's up to you. It will be a long time before we come back and visit all your brothers and sisters again, maybe not until next Christmas."

Pauli uncurled Rosetta's fingers from her hand and hugged Pauline. She whispered tearfully, "I want to go back on the train with you, Aunt Pauline."

Chapter 3

Pauli's Passions

Pauline lived with her unmarried sister, Sallie, in the six-room house their father had built in the Colored section of Durham known as "the Bottoms" because it was located at the bottom of the sloping cemetery where the White citizens of Durham were buried. As the oldest daughter, Pauline was expected to come back

*Grandparents home at 906 Carroll Street in Durham
before the wisteria vines were cut down.*

home and take care of her aging parents when her young husband, Charles Dame, left her to make his way in the White world, never to return.

Charles Dame had studied hard to become a lawyer. After graduating from Howard Law School, he got a good job in a White law office, but it was a struggle for him to find his own clients. He was never able to move up from writing wills and deeds for his White colleagues.

Pauline's husband, Charles Dame, who "passed" as White to pursue a career in law.

One day his good friend John took him aside and said, "Charlie, you'll never get anywhere as a Colored lawyer. But you're as White as any White man. Why don't you cross the color line? Give yourself a better chance in life."

Charles thought long and hard about it. Finally, he sat on their bed one night and watched his wife as she sat at her dresser counting the strokes as she brushed out the silky brown hair she'd inherited from her grandmother Harriet, who was part Cherokee.

"Pauline, don't you see? We have no chance to better ourselves as Colored folk. I want to do what I went to school for, what I worked so hard for. I know I'm smarter than half these fellas who have everything handed to them on a silver plate."

"I know members of both our families have passed," Pauline said. "Especially on my grandmother Sarah Burton's side. A few of the women married Italian men and were never heard from again."

"Your Aunt Marie works in that fancy dress salon in Manhattan as a White woman. She had to do that to get any kind of good job."

"But she lives in Harlem," Pauline countered. "She's only White by day."

"I have a cousin in Philadelphia who is fair-skinned, but his hair is frizzy." Charles smiled, remembering. "He took to wearing a wig to work. One day the wind came along and blew off his wig. There went his job." Charles laughed. "But that wouldn't happen to me. My hair's real, see?" He pulled on his dark blond curls to prove it.

"But, Charles," Pauline reminded him as she began plaiting her hair into long chestnut braids for the night, "we would never be able to see our families. We'd have to live without all their love and support, and sneak into town to see them in the dead of night maybe once a year, like those Simpsons do down the street. My parents would never countenance that. And besides," she argued, "there's so much work to be done for the children. We can't leave them behind."

"You could still teach school, honey. A lot of White women are teaching our children."

"But it has to be done by people of their own kind who can instill them with pride and confidence. I would be playing a charade. Always having to watch myself. And why couldn't you work for social justice in the courts? A lot of those Howard lawyers are doing just that."

"They're not earning their living on a few celebrated court cases. Besides, you know I'm not cut out for that, Pauline. I just want to provide for my family and stay outta trouble."

"Well, Charles, if you have your mind made up, you're going to have to leave *this* trouble behind. Because I can't go with you, darling, I just can't."

Pauline took off her robe and climbed into bed. Charles pulled the covers over her, put his arms around her, and held her until they fell asleep.

And so, Pauline came back home and took up caring for her family the way she always had. Nothing was ever heard from Charles again, though the family sometimes heard stories that he had made a successful career in law in West Virginia.

Aunt Pauline taught school, just as she'd predicted. She taught in the Durham school system in one capacity or another for the next forty-five years. Her school day began at seven thirty in the morning and continued until late at night. She also taught classes to grown-ups who were eager to learn to read now that literacy was no longer forbidden, as it had been during the time of slavery.

Pauli was almost four years old when she came to live with her grandparents and two aunts. Pauline didn't have a plan for how she was going to care for her. She knew her parents were too old to take care of Pauli at home, and her sister Sallie taught school during the day as well. Neither of them could give up working. Their father had a small pension from his service in the Civil War, but it was only enough to pay for the taxes on their one acre of land. Pauline realized she had no choice but to enroll Pauli in school.

The elementary school had three levels of first grade, and usually the children took all three levels before being promoted to second grade. Aunt Pauline taught the highest level, so she asked the principal if Pauli could attend the first-level class. That was fine for about a week, until other parents started clamoring to let *their* young children start school early. Pauli was taken out of the class. Pauline had no choice but to bring her little niece with her into her own classroom. She told Pauli, "You may go and sit with the students at a desk and you may look on while they recite. But you may not recite or play in any of the class games, like the spelling bee. And when you speak to me, don't call me Aunt Pauline, you must call me Mrs. Dame."

One of the games the children played was "Go to the Head of the Class." After a child answered a question incorrectly, the next child in line would take his or her place and that child would go to the end of the line. When the game was over, the child who got all the right answers would remain at the head of the line.

Toward the end of the first year, little Pauli got up to stand in line. Pauline pretended not to see her. She looked in her book to prepare a question for the next student. Pauline saw her niece grab a book from the nearest desk. She opened it up and started reading a sentence aloud from wherever the pages fell. Pauline couldn't help but listen for a moment in wonder. Then she told Pauli quietly but firmly to sit down.

"Yes, Mrs. Dame," Pauli said and did as she was told. She felt ashamed for making such a show of herself. She thought she was in for it when her aunt called her to come forward after class. Instead, Aunt Pauline quietly took another book out of her desk and asked Pauli to read from it aloud. She thought Pauli had memorized what she'd read earlier. Pauli read the new passage without a mistake. Aunt Pauline was amazed that Pauli had been learning along with the other children, even though she wasn't allowed to participate. From that day forward, reading, studying, and searching for knowledge were Pauli Murray's strongest passions and motivations in life.

One of Aunt Pauline's difficulties in raising Pauli was trying to satisfy her ravenous appetite. When Pauli was five years old, Pauline made Pauli's favorite buttermilk pancakes. Pauli waited eagerly for her serving and watched hungrily as her aunt served her grandfather three steaming hotcakes. Then she watched in dismay as Aunt Pauline flipped a single tiny griddlecake onto a plate and placed it in front of her. Pauli felt the sense of injustice and immediate outrage that would always jolt her when confronted by any kind of inequality.

"Aunt Pauline," inquired the little girl, "why did you give Grandfather three pancakes and me only one?"

"Because you're just a little growing girl," Pauline answered. "Look how big Grandfather is compared to you. He has a bigger stomach to fill."

"But how will I ever grow as big as Grandfather if I don't eat as much as I can now?"

Grandfather gave her a sideways smile. "The way food disappears as soon as it is put in front of you, you just might grow up to be as big as me, little Pauli."

It was one thing to be so outspoken at home, but quite another to embarrass Aunt Pauline when they were dinner guests at the home of the Shepherds, one of the most respected families in the community. Pauli eagerly watched Mr. Shepherd's progress as he carved the roast beef at the head of the table, and she was delighted to be served her own grown-up sized portion. After she gobbled it up, Pauli pulled on Aunt Pauline's sleeve and asked, "Aunt Pauline, may I have another slice of meat?"

Pauline's face flushed with embarrassment. She said firmly, "No, dear. You've had quite enough."

Mrs. Shepherd said, "She's welcome to have it, Mrs. Dame." And she added with a hint of pride, "There's plenty of roast beef to go around."

"Mrs. Shepherd, with all due respect," Pauline insisted, "the child needs to learn that 'no' means 'no.'"

"Can I have another piece of meat?" Pauli asked again, oblivious to the tension rising around the table.

"No, you may not, Pauli, and don't ask me again," Aunt Pauline repeated.

"Please," insisted Pauli, "I want another piece of roast beef."

Pauline grew visibly red in the face. Her hair began to curl from the beads of moisture forming on her brow. "Child, I'll take you away from the table and give you a whipping if you ask again." This from Mrs. Dame, the teacher, who never raised her hand to a child. In fact, she went against the grain of most folks of the time and spoke openly against corporal punishment. Her people had suffered too many whippings at the hands of others to be using the rod on themselves, she said. But she also had a naturally timid nature. She never liked to raise her voice or assert herself unnecessarily. So it was doubly hard for her to muster up the resolve to follow through on her threat.

She pulled Pauli up out of her chair and pushed her forward into the parlor, her large hands heavy on Pauli's tiny shoulders. In the dining room, the guests tried to continue their meal without interfering in family discipline. Aunt Pauline laid her niece over her knees and spanked her hard five times with the palm of her hand.

Almost as shaken as Pauli by this episode, she managed to mutter, "Now you'll understand that when I say no, you are to obey me, Miss Pauline Agatha Murray."

When they returned to the table, Pauli showed a stubborn streak that stayed with her in the face of many battles she would face in her life. She sat down in the chair next to her aunt and said, "Aunt Pauline, I want more meat." But Pauline gave her such a severe look that she kept silent for the rest of the meal.

Pauli was so traumatized by that event that she always saved her meat to eat until last on her plate. But there would be times in the future when putting enough food into her small frame was a daunting task.

It came as no surprise when, a little time later, Pauli displayed her passion again. She was with her aunt paying their yearly taxes downtown when they met one of the town's leading White citizens while riding in the elevator to the tax office. The gentleman pulled some change out of his pocket and handed Pauli a nickel.

"And how are you going to spend your money, little girl?"

"I'm going to buy me some beefsteak," Pauli answered.

Pauli's other passion was to avoid any task considered girlish. She preferred running outside with her boy cousins over staying inside dressing up dolls with her girl cousins. At home, she never helped her aunts or grandmother with the cooking or washing. Instead, she split and stacked the firewood for the wood stove that heated their house, fed the chickens, swept the chimney, scrubbed down the outhouse, hoed the garden, and cut the grass around the house with a sickle, taking on men's work the way her aunts had always done on the Fitzgerald farm.

When Pauli was eight years old, she and Aunt Pauline took the train to visit Aunt Rose and Uncle Louis who were taking care of Pauli's brothers and sisters.

"We'll wait to buy you some clothes in Baltimore," Pauline said. "That way we won't have the salespeople staring at us, and we'll be able to use the dressing rooms."

At the store, as they were walking toward the section for girls, they passed the boys' section and Pauli lingered there, fingering the plaid flannel shirts with platinum buttons and eyeing the neatly cuffed navy blue slacks. As Pauline tried to drag her along, she paused at a brown leather jacket with red flannel lining.

"Look at this coat, Aunt Pauline. The leather is so soft and the lining feels real warm. Isn't it handsome?" she asked. "The leather won't get dirty like a wool coat, with me always getting into scrapes the way I do."

Aunt Pauline, "General Sourpuss."

"We can come back and look at it after we check out the coats and dresses in the girls' section."

Pauli begrudgingly settled on a few dresses, but she refused to accept a feminine-style wool coat. Pauli sometimes secretly called her aunt "General Sourpuss" to her Aunt Sallie, who wasn't so strict, but Pauline relented this time and let her niece buy the boys' coat. She even let Pauli bring home a green felt Alpine hat with a feather on the side, which the kids promptly made fun of at school.

At the end of WWI, Pauli laid her hands on a wide-rimmed brown wool hat worn by the infantrymen. Pauline let her wear it wherever she wanted—except to church.

"Child, you will not be wearing that old thing to church unless it's over my dead body," she scolded.

Pauli did so many chores and jobs to earn extra money, she got used to wearing pants when she wasn't in school. At age ten she had her own paper route. She brought the *Carolina Times*, a Black weekly newspaper, to her neighbors on Saturday mornings. From age eleven, she always wore her light brown curly hair in a short bob, the way women were just beginning to do.

"Why you want to wear your hair so short?" her friend Ethel Green asked.

"Because it's more convenient." Pauli shrugged, proud of her choice of words. "I don't have time to be having someone fix my hair up into braids every day."

She had such an air of boyishness, Pauline often referred to her affectionately as "my little boy-girl" to her friends.

Chapter 4

Betwixt & Between

Pauli was looking through the Sears catalogue in the kitchen when she heard the creaking of the wooden steps as Grandfather Robert Fitzgerald came down the worn staircase. She heard him push the screen door open with his cane. She quickly flipped through the pages showing dolls and dresses, and went straight to the section selling outdoor tools and hardware. Half her mind was on the thump, thump of the rocking chair where Grandfather liked to sit on the front porch to hear the sounds of the street. Soon he would bang his cane on the side of the house, a sign that he was ready for her to recite her lessons and read the newspaper to him. Pauli grabbed the small slate board on which she did her figures, stuck the morning newspaper under her arm, and pushed open the screen door.

Just as she expected, Grandfather was leaning back in the rocker with his cane laid across his knees. She watched him take a square of Red Mule tobacco from his pocket and cut himself a plug with his pocketknife. It wasn't easy to tell that the distinguished old gentleman was virtually blind, so deftly did he use his knife and slide it back into his pocket after he was done.

"Are you ready to read that list of words I taught you yesterday?" he began.

"I don't have them written down, Grandfather. I rubbed them off the slate to do the sums you gave me."

"All right, then, you can say them from memory."

Pauli hesitated.

"Well, do you know them or don't you?" Grandfather pressed.

"Yes, I know some of them," Pauli answered.

Grandfather frowned. "How many times have I told you not to say 'yes' when speaking to an older person? Say 'yes sir' or 'yes ma'am' to show your respect. And don't ever let me hear you saying 'yessuh' and 'nossuh' to anybody."

"Yes, sir, Grandfather."

"Now recite those words."

"Am-myu-nish-un, pre-par-ed-ness, al-al-lies," Pauli stammered. "Sub-ma-rine, con-con-scrip-shun."

Grandfather had been a schoolteacher in the days after slavery, when the children couldn't get real schoolbooks. He'd taught the children to read from newspapers and almanacs and, of course, the Bible. "That way, I could kill two birds with one stone," he said. "I taught them something useful while they learned to read."

And that is why Pauli was learning words from the newspaper that were all about the First World War getting ready to start. Grandfather Fitzgerald had served in the Union Army during the Civil War, and he always kept abreast of military news of the day.

Robert Fitzgerald was born outside Wilmington, Delaware, in 1840. His mother, Sara Ann Burton, was from a prosperous White family and his father, Thomas Fitzgerald, was a free man of color. Wilmington was a busy port city on the mail route from Maine to Georgia. It was filled with refugees from the wars in Europe and the potato famine in Ireland. By 1850 only a few property owners still owned slaves in New Castle County. Most of Delaware's two thousand slaves were held in the southern part of the state. And

Delaware had one of the largest populations of free people of color.

Sarah Ann Burton's family were White farmers of French and Swedish heritage who owned land south of Wilmington. As a young man in his twenties, Robert's father, Thomas Fitzgerald, worked for the Burtons as a hired hand and coachman. They valued his hard work and trusted him to make purchases and do other errands that required literacy because he had been taught to read as a boy. In 1834, when the Burtons' eldest daughter, Sarah Ann, turned eighteen, Thomas and Sarah Ann slipped away in the coach and drove to the next town to be married. When they returned home the next day, her parents were so disapproving of their union they sent the two away. But Sarah Ann kept in contact with her younger sisters, Mary Jane and Elizabeth. When the sisters were old enough, they, too, married free men of color—brothers with the last name of Valentine, who were half Black and half White—and went to live with Thomas and Sarah Ann in Wilmington.

Pauli often looked at the picture of Sarah Ann Burton Fitzgerald on the mantelpiece. She could plainly see her great-grandmother was White, yet her descendants now lived in a world that was entirely Black.

The daguerreotype was taken after the Civil War, when Sarah Ann was about fifty years old. She was a stern woman with a grim countenance. Her dark hair was severely parted in the middle and pulled back tightly into a bun. She had to be strong to survive as a White woman in a family subjected to the

Pauli's great-grandmother, Sarah Ann Burton Fitzgerald, 1816-1889.

uncertainty of being both Black and White, and living neither as slaves nor entirely free. Sarah Ann was said to be very outspoken, and her folksy sayings were legendary in the family. She told her children, "If they ask you what you are, just tell 'em that what they see with their eyes, they can't carry off on their noses. Folks is folks and they all look the same in the privy."

Grandfather Robert told a story about a White neighbor coming over one day and saying, "Aint Sary, has any of those no-accounts roun' here been stealing your chickens or your pigs lately? If they have, just let us know and we'll take care of 'em for you." Miz Sarah looked up from weeding the garden and said, "Yes, Uncle, to tell the truth, some of my chickens *have* been missing. The only trouble is, I don't know whether it's White no-accounts or Black no-accounts that's been takin' 'em."

Pauline said, "I guess Sarah Ann needed her sharp tongue. She was always betwixt and between, getting it from both sides of the fence. You see, little Pauli, everybody was so mixed-up and messed-up in those days, you couldn't tell which was which."

Thomas and Sarah Ann managed to bring twelve children into the world, though only six survived. Robert was the third eldest. Because he was quiet and liked to study, his mother trusted him to help with the money she earned on market day. Sarah Ann and Thomas decided that Sarah would be the one to go to market because, as a White woman, she could get a better price for their produce than her husband. Sarah Ann rented a stall near Market House on High Street in Wilmington. She backed her wagon against the curb, unhitched the horse, and sent Robert off to water and graze the horse while she set up her vegetable stall.

Robert loved coming into Wilmington. He loved to stand on the wharf and watch the white sails of vessels moving up and down the Delaware River. One time, he jumped down to the sandy shore and was throwing stones to see if they would glide across the water, when a scrawny White boy in raggedy clothes came down and joined him.

"Do you know how to swim?" the boy asked Robert.

"Sure I do," said Robert. "My pa taught me. He takes me and my brothers down to the bank of the river further up to where we live, and we go fishing."

"I wish my pa would take me fishing. All he does is drink when he's back from the sea."

"Your pa's a sailor?"

"Why, sure. Most everybody I know has a pa what goes to sea."

"I want to be a sailor when I grow up," said Robert. "I want to travel and see places far away, and find buried treasure."

"Ho, you can find pirate's treasure buried along the banks of this very river. My pa found a stash once, but he drank it all up." The boy tossed a rock far out over the water in disgust. "Well, I gotta go now. I hafta be somewhere. I don't suppose you got anything to eat?"

"I think I have a piece of bread." Robert searched his jacket pockets and found a crusty piece. "Here, you can have it."

The boy quickly snatched it from Robert's hand, mumbling, "Thanks," before clambering up the rocks to the street and disappearing behind a passing wagon.

In the winter, Robert walked into town each day to attend the African School on Sixth Street. Most states that still allowed slavery had laws that said it was illegal to teach enslaved people to read and write. It was not against the law in Delaware, but there was no public funding for schools for Black children. When Robert was at the African School, only 187 of more than eighteen thousand free people of color in Delaware were able to go to school.

Robert was chosen to receive an education because he was the frailest of the surviving children. Six of Thomas and Sarah Ann's twelve children had died from tuberculosis or other ailments while they were infants. Robert had survived, but with only one good lung. Even though Robert was the only one going to school, education was a family affair. It was Robert's responsibility to teach his sisters and brothers what he'd learned. When supper was finished, his mother would clear the kitchen table, and Lizzie, Billy, and Richie would gather around the kerosene lamp and lean over Robbie's primer, sounding out the words. Robbie imitated the stern tone and mannerisms of the schoolmaster as he instructed them to recite their ABCs and learn their sums.

But Robert was not the only one in the family who could read. Great-Grandfather Thomas said he had learned to read from the White man who took care of him after his parents died when he was eleven. Every Sunday, Thomas led the family in Bible reading and prayer. Robert remembered those Sundays well, and carried on the tradition in his own family. He told them, "Pa's religion was not the shouting kind; it was a quiet partnership with God, who was

the senior member of our family. As sure as he milked the cows or hoed the corn, Pa made his weekly accounting with the Lord, and we are here to do the same."

Everyone sat quietly while Thomas, Pauli's great-grandfather, slowly read passages from the family Bible. Now and then he would pause to work out a difficult word. When he finished and closed the Bible, all the children, even the youngest, got down on their knees in front of their chairs and bowed their heads.

Pauli's great-grandfather, Thomas Charles Fitzgerald, 1808-1879.

"When Pa began his prayer," Grandfather Robert remembered as he looked with reverence at the daguerreotype of his father in a three-piece suit and cravat, "he talked just as easily and naturally to God as if He were right there in the room and knew every detail of our lives. The prayer started with the family members in the room and moved on to close relatives, and then to relatives far away. He remembered neighbors and friends, from the lowliest vagabond who asked for a place to sleep for the night to the man at the bank who held the mortgage on the farm. Grandfather laughed. "He even remembered the man who tried to buy his crops for less than what they were worth. He would say, 'Lord, let him see his errors and do better next time.'"

Grandfather Robert paused, looking far back into the past before he continued. "As Pa finished praying, everybody joined in to repeat the Lord's Prayer. Each member of the household was made to feel important in the eyes of the Almighty, and that he had his place in the universe."

In 1854, when Robert was fourteen years old, his family was finally able to buy their own land from the money they made selling their produce.

"Listen to this, Miz Sarah," said Thomas as he read the newspaper after dinner. "It says here 'the Pennsylvania legislature has passed a charter,'" he continued slowly, "'a charter to found an institution of learning for the scientific, classical, and theological education of Negro youth of the male sex. The Ashmun Institute is to be located near Hinsonville in Chester County, Pennsylvania.'" He finished reading and said, "That's where we're going to buy our land."

In 1855, Thomas and Sarah rode in their black-curtained Dearborn farm wagon to Upper Oxford township to purchase their farm. Sarah had over two thousand dollars tied up in a cloth around her waist, savings from twenty years of hard work. They were able to purchase a twenty-five-acre farm in cash for $1,632.

As Thomas had learned from careful research, quite a few farmers and homesteaders in Hinsonville were freedmen. The townspeople had a school for their children called Harmony Grove District School. The town also had its own church, built in 1843, called Hosanna Meeting House. Harriet Tubman and Frederick Douglas had spoken there about setting enslaved people free through abolition. Three years before the Fitzgeralds bought their land, there had been a fierce battle in the town of Christiana, fourteen miles west of Hinsonville. The locals called what came to be known as the Christiana Riot "the first battle of the Civil War."

Under the Fugitive Slave Law, any free person of color who didn't have the proper papers could be abducted under the pretext of capturing slaves who had escaped to the freedom of northern states. Many of these former bondsmen and women, who had lived for many years as free people, would be returned to their former condition of servitude. Kidnappers with fake documents rounded up anyone they could catch. Without papers or the witness of White sponsors in the community it was often difficult for people of color to prove they were free.

During a raid near Christiana, a party of slave catchers joined forces with a posse of local White men headed by a US Marshal's deputy. In the early hours before dawn they came to a stone house where a sturdy group of men armed with corn cutters, scythes, clubs, and revolvers stood ready to fight. The men in the posse were the first to flee, but one Maryland slaveowner, who had come with his son to find four runaways missing from his farm, stayed and fought until he was shot in the chest. His wounded son, his own body torn up with bullets, watched his father die.

Thirty-eight men and women were arrested, along with two Quaker men who had refused to join the posse because their religion forbid them to engage in war. The brave men and women who had defended themselves were charged with treason, but the White people in the county were so resentful of slaveowners, they didn't convict a single person.

Because Hinsonville bordered the slave states of Virginia, Maryland, and Delaware, it was an active area of the Underground Railroad, the network that helped people reach freedom in the northern states and Canada. Eighty White families in Chester County operated "stations," or signal posts, on the Underground Railroad. They were good citizens who guided runaways on their treacherous journey to freedom in the North. People escaped into Pennsylvania from Maryland in all kinds of conveyances—hay wagons, oxcarts, broken-down buggies, and sometimes, in coffins riding on a funeral wagon.

One station was manned by a Black man, Abraham D. Shadd, who harbored fugitives on his own farm. Most Black freedmen couldn't afford to take such a risk. Yet, they helped in many ways. The Hosanna Quaker Meeting House was an important outpost of the Underground Railroad. Runaways often made their escape on Sundays because they were given their own time from Saturday night until Monday morning. If they could reach Hosanna Meeting House during Sunday Meeting, they would mingle with the congregation and hitch a ride, hidden in the wagon of a family on their way home from church.

Once the Fitzgeralds settled in Hinsonville, there always seemed to be unfamiliar Black men or women who came along asking to sleep in the barn. Thomas Fitzgerald never asked their names or what their business was.

"Don't tell me anything about yourself," Thomas would tell them. "Just mind yourself and don't set my barn afire. If you're here in the morning, you'll get breakfast. If you leave before day, you'll find your tobacco and pipe on the ledge by the barn door as you go out."

Seeing that construction of the new Ashmun Institute was about to begin, Thomas Fitzgerald formed a partnership with owners of a nearby brickyard. He bought a second horse and wagon, and hauled the dirt and stones that laid the foundation for the school buildings. His three sons apprenticed in the brickmaking trade while still keeping up with the farming. And Robert still had his schooling to attend to.

"I used to drive my father's oxen along a furrow with a book in one hand," Grandfather Robert told little Pauli when she didn't seem sufficiently motivated to study. "When I wasn't studying, I drew sketches in a small notebook I always carried in my pocket. I took that notebook to the battlefield with me. I still have those diaries I scribbled in during the War for Emancipation. They're locked away in your grandmother Cornelia's desk upstairs."

When he was sixteen, Robert entered the Institute for Colored Youth, sponsored by the Quakers. It was the only secondary school for people of color. From there he went on to the Ashmun Institute, which his family had helped build with bricks made by their own hands. After the war, the school was renamed the Lincoln Institute, and eventually became Lincoln University.

Chapter 5

Civil War Enlistment

It was a wintry night in Durham, North Carolina, and the Fitzgeralds were reading the evening's Bible lesson. A warm fire was gently smoldering in the fireplace. Aunt Pauline was correcting some papers at the table and Aunt Sallie was doing some mending. They were reading the lessons about the battle of Galilee, and Grandfather had murmured something about the heat of the battle from his own experience.

"Grandfather, tell us again about when you were in the battle of St. Petersburg in the Civil War," Pauli pleaded. "Please, sir."

Grandfather gazed up at the ceiling as though listening to the far-off blaring of bugles calling soldiers to pick up their guns. Then he began to tell his story.

"Almost as soon as the first shots were fired in the Civil War, I was eager to enlist. We were thoroughly demoralized by the Dred Scott decision, passed a few years before. The highest court of the land denied the right to citizenship for anyone with African ancestry. In our eyes, this made our status as free colored folk seem barely a step away from slavery. We knew that if we could only fight for the Union cause as brave soldiers alongside the Whites, we would finally achieve real citizenship. So I went with my two brothers, Billy and Richie, along with a few fellow students from Ashmun Institute and some other young men from Hinsonville, to the nearest recruiting office to sign up when President Lincoln called for seventy-five thousand able-bodied men to serve for three months when the war began.

"We lined up next to local White farmers and laborers who had just emigrated from Germany, men who spoke hardly a word of English. We were mortified when the Negro men were the only ones told to return home. They were not going to take Colored men. The whole county was stripped of its young White men. Folks used to hurl insults at us when my brothers and I were walking along the road. You see, we were often taken for White because we had such light complexions.

"'Hey, Yank,' the old geezers in town who didn't know us would yell. 'Whyn't you joined up with the troops?'

"We just shrugged and kept walking, not wanting a confrontation.

"'You must be damned doughfaces, or secessionists,' they taunted.

"Billy said, 'Listen, they think we're White. Why don't we just go sign up as White boys?'

"Richie added, 'That's right. A lot of boys are doin' it. They sign up as Indian, Irish, or Italian. Long as you don't look Black, they don't ask questions.'

"'You know Pa would never stand for that,' I told them. As the oldest, I had to have the voice of reason. 'Pa always says, Never be ashamed of what you are. Just be the best you can be and show what we can do when given the chance.'

"'That's right,' said Richie, the fighting one. 'I'm not going to go into battle and show my bravery and let the Whites take the credit. If I'm going in, it's going to be for the credit of the Negro race.'

"'Besides,' said Billy, 'you'd have to act like one of them, hearing all their insults and jokes about our people and having to join in on the laughs. That would sicken my heart.'

"When we got home, Pa told us he'd heard news that the quartermasters who handled the supplies were looking for civilians to join up. 'The Union needs teamsters, wagon masters, mule drivers, and hostlers for the long wagon trains to supply the army for the Bull Run Campaign. They're looking for wheelwrights and blacksmiths, and men to build roads and bridges. Laborers get twenty dollars a month, teamsters get twenty-five, and a wagon master gets thirty-five. There's a recruiting office at Fifth and Walnut Street in Philadelphia.'

"Pa got work as a teamster and assistant wagon master during the winter months when he didn't have to tend to farming. Richard spent most of that year driving mules around Harrison's Landing and Fortress Monroe. Billy drove a one-horse cart at Aquia Creek. I worked in a construction corps building roads and pontoon bridges.

"I did most everything. I chopped down trees, drove a six-mule team in the wagon train, sometimes served as company cook for the regiment. The wagon wheels often broke and got stuck in the mud. I delivered horses to Antietam, Culpeper, and to Warrentown, Virginia. Working for the quartermasters meant you didn't get to wear a uniform or carry a gun. Men of all kinds were enlisted in the quartermaster service. They would take anybody they could get, as long as he walked on two legs. There were strange men from the mountains, drunks and thieves and many runaways.

"It was said they hired the Negroes for the lowest kind of work, so more of the White soldiers could carry out strictly military assignments. They thought they'd imitate the Southern soldiers who took their slaves along with them to serve as valets."

Grandfather laughed bitterly to tell this part of his story. "Many of the men I worked with at my side were runaways who had escaped and joined regiments to do whatever they could for the cause. These men were called contraband since they were the so-called property of the enemy. But these men came to the Union army with maps and supplies and good information about the enemy troops.

"One day, I was doing chores around the wagon near the creek when I heard a rustling in the bushes. What did I see but a whole family of desperate Negroes coming up out of the water over the bank of the creek."

"Where did they come from?" asked Pauli.

"They came from a plantation that had been overrun by the Union army. The man wanted to stay and get work, but I persuaded him to go on with his family. He had a pregnant wife and two forlorn children in tow. I did what I could to warm them and feed them and send them on their way up North with what supplies I could spare."

"And when did the Emancipation Proclamation come?" asked Aunt Sallie, to keep the story going.

"That was another disappointment. When President Lincoln finally signed the Emancipation Proclamation, it did not free the slaves in the loyal border states. Only the slaves of the secessionist states were freed. Mr. Lincoln was calling for Negroes to go back to a place in Africa they called Liberia." Grandfather scoffed. "I remember at the Ashmun Institute they trained missionaries to go to Liberia, and they asked me to join them, but I would have none of that back-to-Africa palaver. Negroes built up this country same as everybody else and we deserve a place here."

"And what happened at Harper's Ferry, Father?" Aunt Pauline spurred her father to continue.

"Well," said Grandfather, rubbing his chin, "I was traveling at night, transferring horses from Harper's Ferry on the Potomac River near Point of Rocks. I heard musket shots and tried to hide by scrambling down an embankment with my horses. But I couldn't escape a bullet that struck the rim of my left eye. The bullet shattered a piece of the bone and embedded itself behind my eyeball. I do believe I fainted dead away. Next thing I knew I was in a hospital, totally blind."

"But your blindness didn't come during the war, Father," Aunt Sallie remembered.

"I'd had bouts of blindness before. It reminded me of times when I was a boy and would have a case of night blindness as a result of my battle with tuberculosis. I remember one time that happened, I was coming back from school, walking home late in the evening. I lost my way and veered off the road. I was reduced to crawling in the woods until I finally found the direction of the road by hearing a wagon drive by."

"But tell us what happened in the hospital during the war," Grandmother Cornelia insisted, putting down her sewing to hear the story again.

"The orderly told me, 'If you don't get your sight back soon, we may have to operate, but you may lose your sight altogether if we try to take the bullet out.' I prayed hard to the good Lord for my sight to return. Two weeks later, by a miracle, I was able to see again."

"Praise the Lord," said Cornelia, shaking her head.

"By then the doctors had no time for operations, and I was discharged," Grandfather continued. "But throughout the winter my eyesight faded on many occasions. Many times I had to grope around and guess at the whereabouts of things to fulfill my duties." He rubbed the left side of his head. "I can still feel that bullet in my temple."

"When did you get your citizenship, Father?" Aunt Pauline asked, though she'd heard the story many times before.

"Finally, the attorney general issued an opinion that a free person of color, if they were born in the United States, was a citizen. But we were still not allowed to enlist in the United States Army and serve our country, even though the Emancipation Proclamation allowed former slaves to enlist. Massachusetts was the first state to sign up Negro recruits, and they came from everywhere to sign up. But Pennsylvania was still balking.

"So, I came back to Pennsylvania to rest up my wound and wait to see if Pennsylvania would start recruiting Colored men. My cousin Joe Valentine and I were waiting at the post office to hear some word when a bundle of newspapers was thrown down and we ran over to grab one. The governor was still holding out for a state of emergency before he would let us sign up. But I noticed another story, about the pay of Negroes already enlisted in the Fifty-Fourth and Fifty-Fifth Massachusetts Regiments and traveling south.

"I remember the notice said, 'Secretary of War Staunton has ruled that Negro soldiers will get ten dollars a month plus three dollars' worth of clothing.' Well, we knew the White soldiers were getting thirteen dollars a month, and got their clothing free. The governor of Massachusetts had already said, when he was enlisting Negro soldiers, they would get equal pay. I decided then and there I wasn't going to join any army that didn't treat all soldiers alike.

"My cousin Joe said, 'I hear the Navy takes all comers. If an escaped slave is taken on a ship, they're putting him to work and payin' 'em equal too! And they're enlisting men right now in New York City.'

"So Joe and me, we set out for the Brooklyn Navy Yard and signed up. Our pay was sixteen dollars a month," Grandfather said proudly. "The first thing I did when I got my uniform was go straight to a photographer's studio and have my portrait taken."

Grandfather Robert Fitzgerald in his U.S. Navy uniform in 1863, 1840-1919.

"And here it is, Grandfather," said Pauli, jumping up and running to the mantlepiece where she picked up the old tintype that had been displayed there for as long as she could remember. She looked admiringly at the picture of Grandfather as a jaunty young man of twenty-two. He had a handsome face with a small, carefully trimmed mustache and was dressed in a short Navy jacket with a kerchief tied loosely in front. His round sailor's cap was tipped jauntily toward his right eyebrow and a metal identification tag hung from a cord about his neck.

"What was the Navy like, Grandfather? Were you glad you finally got to go to sea?" Pauli asked from her perch on a wooden stool by his knee.

"Before we were allowed out to ship out, we trained on a Navy ship at the Brooklyn Navy Yard. We learned deck drills, steering, rowing, knotting and splicing ropes, climbing riggings, bending and reefing sails, and manning and firing nine-inch and twelve-pound guns aboard the training ship. Then I was assigned to a ship called the *Ossippee* that was sailing to New Orleans. But enough war stories for tonight. You all need to get a good night's rest to rise up early and get ready for school."

Grandfather probably didn't want to talk too much about his Navy service. In truth, he never saw combat and spent most of his time pumping out leaks in the engine room and fetching coal in a small dinghy on choppy seas from a supply ship that was standing by. He never told his family about the time he was put in double irons and fed bread and water for five days for "insolence."

When Pauli grew up, she found the incident recorded in the ship's log of September 29, 1863. Eventually Robert fell sick with malaria. His periodic blindness came back and he was released from service on January 14, 1864. Yet the very next day, he signed up to serve in the Third Negro Regiment mustered by the governor of Massachusetts. He lied about his discharge from the Navy and the recruiting office wasn't conducting any vision tests. After many harrowing adventures, which he recorded in a personal diary lovingly handed down to his family, he contracted typhoid fever. Again, his blindness returned and he was honorably discharged on October 4, 1864. He learned that his regiment was one of the first to march into Richmond, Virginia in the spring of 1865.

Chapter 6

Baltimore

Aunt Pauline placed the old sepia portrait photographs of Pauli's parents on the mantelpiece, so Pauli would not forget them. She told her niece stories about Agnes and Will to make her proud that she came from two bright, accomplished people. They used to play a game about it.

"Who am I like today, Aunt Pauline?" Pauli would ask her aunt as she studied her lessons at the kitchen table after the evening meal.

"You've got your mother's sweet disposition today," Aunt Pauline would say.

When Aunt Pauline heard Pauli recite a poem she'd learned in school, she said, "As I watched you reciting, you looked just like your father. I saw Will Murray all over again."

Aunt Pauline also told stories about the Murray sisters and brothers: Mildred, Grace, Will Jr., and the two younger children, Raymond and Rosetta. When Pauli learned her aunt had finally saved enough money to make the train trip to Baltimore to see her father and her brothers and sisters, she was overjoyed. It had been five years since they'd returned to Maryland—since Agnes had died. Grandmother Cornelia made fried chicken especially for the trip.

Aunt Pauline reserved two berths in a private Pullman railcar where they could sleep overnight and not have to sit in seats reserved for African Americans. According to the segregation laws, public accommodations for Whites and Blacks had to be separated in Southern states that had engaged in slavery before the Civil War. These ordinances, originally called "black codes," were intended to roll back laws granted by the Fourteenth Amendment after the war. The new restrictions prevented African American citizens from voting, serving on juries, and running for political office. To demean African Americans who aspired to become middle-class citizens, the White southerners labeled these laws after a character popularized in a song called "Jump Jim Crow" from the 1830s.

In the Pullman car, Pauli could hardly sleep from excitement, feeling the rumbling of the train as it plummeted through the starry night. She was especially looking forward to seeing her father. Even though he was in the hospital because of a recurrence of his illness, Aunt Pauline had promised they would visit him.

Baltimore was a real city, much bigger than Durham. Pauli was fascinated by the rows and rows of identical houses with no porches or yards, just concrete steps leading to the front door from the sidewalk. Aunt Rose and Uncle Lewis Murray lived in a large three-story house with a basement. Their furnishings were fashionable and elegant, and they wore the latest styles of clothing. When they arrived, Pauli's eldest sister, Mildred, who was fifteen now, quickly opened the door when she heard their steps on the landing. After a few rounds of hugs they were led into the parlor where Aunt Rose waited for them in her maroon horsehair armchair. She was so plump she didn't like to walk if she didn't have to. Her orange hair was swept up in a great bun and her face and arms were covered in freckles. She spent most of her time shouting orders to Pauli's sisters to make sure they did their chores and whatever else she wanted done at the moment.

"Mildred, go bring in the cookies you all made this morning. And, Grace, bring the lemonade in those pretty glasses. Fresh squeezed by Willie this morning," she added. "My goodness," she said to Pauline,

"I don't know what I would do without these children to help me. They are such a help to Uncle Lewis and me, with Lewis working so hard teaching at the high school."

Just then, Uncle Lewis came in dressed in a fancy dark blue, pin-striped suit with an ascot at the neck.

"Well, look at you, little Pauli," Uncle Lewis laughed, grabbing his niece by the shoulders. "I remember when you were just a wee little thing. And look at you now, all grown up. Turn around. Let me get a good look at you." He sized her up and down, making Pauli feel shy and uncomfortable. "Looks like you're growing out of that dress too. It'll be time you wear longer dresses right soon," he instructed her, scrutinizing her so closely she thought he would say something about her socks and shoes.

Some of the neighbors stopped by and Aunt Rose introduced Pauli as her child. "This here is little Pauli," she announced, pushing Pauli forward. "She's another one of my children who has been living down South." Aunt Pauline didn't say anything, but Pauli could see the color start to rise in her cheeks. Later that night, when Mildred and Pauli were in bed together, Pauli asked her sister, "Why did Aunt Rose say I was one of her children? I'm no more her child than you are! We're Agnes and Will's children."

"Mother doesn't like any of us even to talk about our real mother and father. She says that's all in the past and we don't have to worry about that anymore. Why, Rosetta and Raymond are forbidden even to know that Mother isn't their real mother."

"How can Aunt Rose be your *real* mother when she is your *father's* sister?" Pauli argued.

"I know that, but Aunt Rose doesn't want us to tell the younger children."

The next day Pauli was playing catch in the yard with little Raymond and Rosetta when Raymond suddenly asked her, "How come you're livin' with Aunt Pauline if you're our sister?"

Pauli bounced the ball and tried to ignore him, but inside she was hurt and confused. She knew she shouldn't tell the children something that would only hurt them, but she couldn't help herself—she must speak the truth. "Don't you know our real mother is dead?" she finally said. "Aunt Pauline adopted me just like Aunt Rose adopted you. Aunt Rose is really your aunt, just like Pauline is my aunt, even though she is my adoptive mother."

"That's not true," Rosetta wailed, her eyes opening wide in disbelief.

"You're a fat liar," countered Raymond.

"I am not." To prove it, she said, "How can Aunt Rose be your real mother when she's your father's sister? And your real name is Robert, after our grandfather, Robert Fitzgerald—who you don't even know," she added indignantly.

Raymond and Rosetta ran into the house, straight to Aunt Rose, and clung to her skirts, telling her this wicked story.

"Pauline," Aunt Rose called out in her high-pitched voice. "You come straight in here. You ought to be ashamed of yourself, young lady, upsetting my children like this. You come right over here to get you a whipping."

But Aunt Pauline came into the room and stopped her, saying, "No, Rose, I can't let you punish her for telling the truth."

Pauli stood defiantly in front of Aunt Rose, exhibiting the stubbornness that would follow her the rest of her life, for good or ill, she was not always sure.

"Then you must apologize for what you've done. To be so mean-spirited."

"I won't," Pauli stammered.

"You will if you know what's good for you."

But Pauli refused until finally Aunt Rose ordered her upstairs to stay in her room, and Pauline didn't interfere. Pauli climbed all the way up to the attic room she shared with Mildred underneath the sloping roof. She slammed the door tight behind her and climbed into bed, tears wetting her pillow as she fell asleep. Finally, Aunt Rose sent Raymond upstairs to say she could come down for dinner. When she tried to open the door, it wouldn't budge. Pauli had shut it so hard it was stuck.

"Mama, Pauli's door won't open. She's locked in her room," Raymond called down the stairs.

Rose took a while to raise herself from the couch. She waddled into the hall and called up from the bottom of the stairs. "What are you saying, young man?"

"Pauli's gone and locked herself in."

"Are you telling me the truth, boy?" Aunt Rose shouted. "You want me to come all the way up these stairs to open that door? Lordy, Lordy, what a trial that girl is." Rose huffed and puffed her way up the stairs, stopping every few steps to catch her breath. Once at the top, she jangled the doorknob without success. Then she pushed all of her considerable weight against the door, and it flew open. Pauli ducked past her and ran down the stairs.

The next hurdle came when they visited Pauli's father, Will, in the state hospital where his brother Lewis had him committed due to his violent moods. Mildred whispered the whole story to Pauli as they lay in bed one night.

"Father and Aunt Rose didn't get along at all. Aunt Rose didn't like Father coming to visit us, and they got into arguments. Aunt Rose and Uncle Lewis tried to visit him to bring him food, but he didn't even want them to come to where he lived. He would tell me, 'Mildred, tell them not to visit me anymore. They just want to meddle in my affairs. Tell them you'll bring me anything they have for me.'

"After another argument, one of our cousins had the police pick him up and they had him signed in to the crazy hospital. We're not allowed to go see him there. If you and Aunt Pauline go, please take me with you. I want to see Father. I miss him so."

"Sure, you can go with us," Pauli said. "You're the oldest, anyway. You were always Father's favorite." But Pauli underestimated the will of Aunt Rose. When they were getting ready to leave, she barred the door with her enormous body and said, "Mildred, you will go with them to the hospital over my dead body. I don't want my daughter experiencing any unnecessary sorrow about things she can't help. Seeing that man in his condition—it's not right."

So Aunt Pauline took Pauli's hand and marched out of the house to go see her brother-in-law, Will.

On the train to Annapolis, Pauli pestered her aunt with questions.

"Will Father be happy to see me?" she asked.

"He will, dear."

"Do you think he'll really remember me?"

"I'm sure he will, but you've grown up so much in five years."

"Of course he will," said Pauli, "because everybody says I look so much like him. I want to tell him all about school and that I'm becoming just as smart as him."

"As smart as *he is*," Pauline corrected.

"I'll tell him that I made the honor roll in my class this spring."

When they got to the station, they walked along the track in the direction of the state hospital, following the steady stream of people going to visit their relatives. When they reached the unadorned concrete building they were led into a dim waiting area with long benches lined up in the middle of the room. There were no pictures on the dingy walls. They watched patiently as men in freshly starched overalls came into the room one by one. They were each greeted with hugs and laughter. Then they went outside to the grounds with their families to share a picnic lunch. But there was no sign of Will Murray.

"Mother, where is he? Why isn't Father coming? Can I go look in the window to see if he is on his way?" She ran to the door and stood on her tiptoes to peer through the window. She saw an old man coming down the hallway, moving slowly in an old pair of boots that were cracked and worn. He hardly picked up his feet as he walked. Pauli was disappointed it wasn't Father. This man was wearing old, faded overalls with threadbare patches on the knees. His hair was uncombed, he had a few days' growth of beard, and his eyes looked dull. Pauli backed up to let him go past. She heard Aunt Pauline take in her breath behind her.

"Is it Will?" Pauline asked in dismay, her voice almost a whisper.

"What's left of me," the man answered, standing with his hands hanging down at his sides. "I almost didn't come. I don't like to see the family anymore. They didn't tell me it was you, Sister Pauline. I'm so glad to see you."

"Pauli, come over here. This is Will, your father."

Pauli walked slowly up to her father, and stared. "He doesn't look like my father," she said quietly.

"No, I don't suppose I do," the man answered. "Are you my little girl?" William's voice softened as he knelt down to be the same height as his daughter. "I haven't seen any of my children in such a long time, I don't know who I would recognize. Mildred? Grace?"

"It's me, Pauli."

"Oh, my little one who was so smart. You went down to live with Sister Pauline. I remember you now."

William sat down on the bench and let out a long sigh. "I'm sorry you have to see me like this. They give us new overalls to wear when we have visitors, but I got into an argument this morning and this is how they punished me. I'd have tried to stay out of trouble if I knew you were coming. You know, my temper sometimes gets the better of me."

"How are they treating you, Will?" his sister asked.

William leaned over and spoke softly. "I want to get out of here. Anything could happen. The guards are worse than the patients for picking fights. They tell me I'm well enough to go, but I need someone to sign me out."

Pauline didn't know what to say. She knew she couldn't help him get back on his feet again. The guard came and said the visiting hour was just about up. They gave him the basket of food they'd brought him. He looked through the basket and found a packet of cigarettes

Pauline had wrapped up in a napkin. He smiled gratefully and thanked her. After they said their goodbyes, Pauline heard him say, almost to himself, "Time passes by you in a place like this, and one day is just like another."

In keeping with Aunt Pauline and Pauli's dismal mood, it was storming when they left the hospital, a huge storm that affected the whole East Coast. Lightning struck their passenger car and they had to wait an hour before they were moved to another. To add to their sorrow, when they finally got back to the Murrays, there was a telegram waiting for them from Grandmother. Grandfather Fitzgerald was ill and Grandmother Cornelia didn't think he had much time left. They had to leave immediately to go back to Durham.

They quickly packed their bags, but there was no one to drive them to the train station a mile away in the rain. Mildred and Grace walked with them, to help carry their bags. They hurried along in the last drizzling of the storm, trudging over the old cobblestone streets, the round bricks slick from the rain. Suddenly, Aunt Pauline slipped and fell, making a sharp cry as she tumbled onto the rough stones. Her glasses shattered as her head struck the pavement, and she lay quietly for a full minute, stunned and unable to move.

Her face was bloody where the lens of her glasses had been crushed into her cheek. Mildred and Grace instinctively looked around for help. They saw two White men standing nearby, engaged in conversation and having a smoke. The girls looked toward them for help, but even though the men stopped talking and looked toward them, when they caught the girls' gaze, they turned away.

Grace and Mildred were able to lift Pauline to her feet after she regained her senses. "Come on now, young ladies, you can help this old woman up," she encouraged them, even in her weakened state.

They gathered up their suitcases and scattered packages, and continued on to the station.

"Are you all right, Mother?" Pauli asked her aunt.

"I'll be all right," she answered, though she could barely see without her glasses. "You'll have to be my eyes on this journey, Pauli." And then, more to herself, she added, "To think, those two White men saw how helpless we were and they just stood right there without making a move to help us."

They were not able to reserve a Pullman car on such short notice, so they entered the segregated car with their spirits sinking. Pauli saw how different the segregated coach accommodations were. They were seated in the car closest to the engine. The door was left open and red-hot cinders flew from the engine right into the car.

Because of the bad weather, they couldn't buy their tickets straight through to Durham. They would have to stop in Norfolk to detour around the effects of the storm, which had damaged the tracks. They arrived in Norfolk late at night, with only the two of them now to carry their suitcases—a forty-seven-year-old woman and a ten-year-old girl. No one in the nearly deserted station offered to help the struggling pair. They stopped, exhausted, at the entrance to the waiting room, dropping their bundles right there.

"Can you see where the ticket window is, Pauli?"

"It's way down at the other end of the station, Aunt Pauline."

"I'm going to leave you here, darling, with our bags, while I go purchase the tickets to Durham."

The station was dark and quiet, and the longer it took Aunt Pauline to get the tickets, the more uncomfortable and nervous Pauli became. A little ways away, she could feel the unpleasant gaze of a tall, hefty White man. He had a big red face and a fat nose. Pauli was careful and looked down at the floor. She knew she was not supposed to greet White people unless they spoke first, nor look them straight in the eye.

As Pauli looked down, she suddenly saw the man's large boots planted right in front of her. He stared down at her and began to scratch his head with a perplexed expression. He motioned to his companions to come over, and soon all three were standing over Pauli, studying her intently. The men didn't say anything, just shrugged their shoulders dramatically with expressions of bewilderment, shaking their heads and looking at each other as if she wasn't even there. She stood locked to the spot, not daring to look up, afraid they might suddenly strike her.

Soon, Aunt Pauline marched through those men and spoke to Pauli pointedly. "Come along, darling. I've got the tickets. The train is waiting for us on the platform. We can go aboard now."

The men stood back as the woman and her child gathered their numerous packages as best they could and hurried out of the waiting room. They climbed up into the car reserved for Colored. Only half the car had proper seats. The rest of the car was stuffed with the baggage for all the other passengers on the train. As they settled into their seats, Aunt Pauline still worried what further trouble that man in the waiting room might cause.

The door to the car suddenly flew open and the burly White man pushed his way inside. Pauli and her aunt were the only people in the car, but he made a point of coming up close to them and staring. He looked them up and down as if confirming his suspicions before turning around and stepping out of the car.

"Aunt Pauline, why is that man so concerned with us?"

"Darling, it never ceases to amaze me the lengths to which some people will go. Because I don't have my glasses, I made the mistake of setting you down in the Whites Only waiting room. Those men stood over you wondering what you were doing in the Whites Only area. Once he figured out who we were, he came into our car to make sure we had boarded the proper car."

Aunt Pauline sighed. "Norfolk didn't have segregated waiting rooms the last time I came through here, fifteen years ago, to visit your mother. Lord, sometimes I don't know if the world is changing for the better or the worse." For Pauli's sake, she brightened. "All we can do is trust in the Lord and better ourselves in hopes of a better future to come."

Chapter 7

Grandmother Cornelia

After Grandfather died, Grandmother Cornelia's fear of the night came back to torment her. She didn't feel safe without him, even though he was an old man, as good as blind. She began to wake up and pace the house on a regular basis. It was keeping Aunt Pauline up at night, and she needed her rest to be ready for the next day's classes.

"I declare, I'm going to have to go stay with my sister if she keeps this up. I can't get a bit of sleep with her prowling around and moving furniture all over her room at night."

Finally, Aunt Pauline went to live with Aunt Sallie and her new husband at the Rectory of the Episcopal church, where he was the pastor. But they couldn't leave Grandmother Cornelia alone, so it was decided that Pauli, only eleven years old,

Grandmother Cornelia Smith Fitzgerald, 1844-1924.

would sleep in her grandmother's room until Cornelia settled down and came out of her spell.

The house Grandfather Fitzgerald built for them in Durham was at the bottom of a hill, on land that butted right up next to a graveyard. That was scary enough, but the house was past the part of the road lit by street lamps, isolated from other houses. Grandmother was so nervous about intruders, every evening when night started to fall and the shadows lengthened across the yard, she began her ritual of locking and barricading all the windows and doors downstairs.

She locked the front door and the back door, pushing their bolts tight. She placed crossbars across the kitchen window and the windows in the parlor next to the porch. She was too afraid to stay in the kitchen to prepare dinner. She set an oil lamp on the landing above the stairs so she and Pauli could see their way. Then they would bring everything they needed for the evening up to her bedroom. They brought all the food and dishes and a pail of water to wash them in, and they carried another bucket up for their waste.

It wasn't enough to be upstairs—Cornelia pushed the table and chairs against the bedroom door. She pushed a basket of clothing against the window and piled boxes above it so nothing could be seen from outside. Rather than save themselves from any fire, should one occur, they were sure to be smothered. Next, Cornelia hauled Grandfather's Civil War weapons out of the trunk. She pulled out his musket, his bayonet, and his saber, and placed all these instruments of war under her bed, adding the axe she used for chopping wood. Then she went to her dresser and pulled a pearl-handled revolver out of the bottom drawer and placed it under her pillow.

"Do you have bullets for that gun, Grandmother?" young Pauli asked warily.

"No, I don't, but they don't know that. I don't know if they even make bullets for this old pistol anymore, but it'll sure put the fear of God in anybody who tries to bring us harm."

There was a fireplace in the bedroom and Pauli helped her grandmother get the fire started with wood she'd carried in from outside. "What are you going to make for dinner, Grandmother?" Pauli asked, though she already knew it was going to be the simplest meal. How she missed Pauline's gravy over hot biscuits, and apple pie for dessert.

"I'll be roasting these potatoes you brought up from the bin downstairs," Cornelia said. "I'm going to set these collards that survived the frost in the garden to boil with this salt pork, and we'll stir up some cornmeal to fry up in this skillet here. That should be a fine enough meal for the likes of us."

Pauli tried to get a little of her homework done, but Grandmother's fear was contagious, and every time she heard the slightest noise, Pauli would lose her concentration and imagine that Grandmother might be right—there really were prowlers out there who wanted to come in and rob them, or maybe worse. As soon as she could, she changed out of her school clothes and jumped into her grandmother's big bed with the feather mattress, covering her head with the warm coverlet, hoping to fall asleep while Grandmother was still tidying up from the meal.

Every night about midnight, Grandmother would start to hear things, and would marshal up her defenses. Pauli would wake up to the sound of heavy scraping on the bare floor under the bed. Grandma was pulling the axe out and dragging it across the floor to prepare for the intruders.

"You get away from here, you devils!" she'd shout. "If you don't, I'm going to pour a kettle of scalding water down on your heads."

Cornelia would be silent for a while, listening, then she would start up again, pounding on the floorboards with the handle of the axe. She carried on this way until she finally put the axe back under the bed and pulled the coverlet over her, exhausted from her travails. By then Pauli was wide awake herself, hearing the slightest creak of the floorboards and feeling as though she might jump out of her skin. If the limb of the tree scraped against the house in the wind, that would be enough to keep her awake until dawn.

Grandmother Cornelia had reason to be afraid. She had fearsome memories of long ago, living in an isolated cabin out in the dense woods of Orange County, North Carolina, near the town of Chapel Hill. She had inherited a small farm from her aunt, Mary Ruffin Smith, her father's sister, the White slave-owning spinster who had raised her. Mary Smith gave Cornelia the hundred-acre farm when she and Robert Fitzgerald were married. Cornelia often stayed alone to look after the farm while Robert took their children to Durham to work in his brickyard.

In 1869, General Ulysses S. Grant, who had led the Union Army in the Civil War, was elected president, and the Fitzgeralds moved to North Carolina looking for new opportunities. They believed they could put their skills in brickmaking to good use with the need for new buildings caused by the devastation from the war. Robert also wanted to fulfill the great need for educators, teaching in the new schools for freedmen and freedwomen, and their children.

Thomas and Sarah Ann Fitzgerald had saved up enough money in Pennsylvania to purchase an abandoned plantation outside of Durham. They paid twelve hundred dollars cash for 158 acres that included a two-story house, a small cottage, and a few cows and oxen. After Thomas died, Sarah couldn't manage the place alone so she moved closer to Durham, and Robert and Cornelia built a house on the land that Cornelia had inherited.

When they were old enough, Robert often took his five daughters and one son to help out at the brickyard, leaving Cornelia alone to care for the farm. Robert used to say, "What my daughters lacked in brawn, they made up for in zeal and agility. Why, my daughters could plow, load hay, work a farm, and lay brick as well as their brother Tommie." He told Pauli, "There are four things every woman should know how to do: ride, shoot, drive a horse, and row a boat."

After the war, the White men who wanted to make sure the freed people didn't make any gains in life were joining a secret organization, the Ku Klux Klan. They intended to run Black farmers off their land, especially those who were doing well for themselves.

One day, a White storekeeper stopped Robert's brother Billy in front of a group of farmers passing the time on a Saturday afternoon. "What'll you folks do down on that farm you got if the Kluxers pay you a visit?"

Billy stuck out his chest a bit and made a little laugh. "Well, I don't reckon there's much we can do. We don't have more'n ten or twelve guns and a few rounds of ammunition. But I can tell you one thing, if the Ku-Kluxers do come, they won't all come back."

After that, the situation got so tense for Billy, even with his bravado, he became discouraged and decided to return to Pennsylvania. The rest of the family endured many nights staying up with their guns by their sides, listening to the clatter of hooves as the hooded Klansmen rode past their farm. In the early years after the war, Federal troops were called in to settle things down, but now they were gone and the threat was always present.

Grandmother Cornelia remembered a time years later, after the troops had been removed as a result of the 1877 Compromise and after President Grant left office: Cornelia was home alone late at night when the hooded men rode out to the isolated farmhouse. At first, Cornelia heard the clatter of their horses' hooves on the road. She thought they would pass on. Their whooping and whistling was enough to wake the dead in the silent woods. But as the shouting got louder, she knew they were coming up the rutted lane to the house. She didn't dare look outside. She didn't want to know how many were out there and whether they were carrying lighted torches or not. The men circled the cabin, riding 'round and 'round it with the roar of the horses' hooves pounding on the mud and dirt in the yard sounding like thunder in a furious storm. They shouted their taunting insults up to her window.

"Corneely Smith think she so high and mighty. Bastard daughter of Sidney Smith or his brother Frank, who knows? The two of them had their way with her Injun mammy whenever it suited them. Didn't know whose kids they were. And ol' Mary Ruffin Smith never married. So hard up, she thought to raise those pickaninnies in her own house. Now look at Miz Corneely, think she somethin' 'cause she got a few dirt acres what nothin' grows on. How long you want to stay out here, Missy? Where your husband at? Ain't he gonna come outside and protect you with his old musket?"

Their taunting went on and on. Cornelia knelt down by the side of her bed, her hands clasped together, shaking her head and praying, looking up toward the heavens. "Oh, please, Lord, just don't let me die a burning death. Take me quickly, let my heart stop. Have mercy on me, Lord. And thank you for sparing my husband and children. Just take me quickly. Don't let them burn me to death."

She told Pauli she didn't know how long she prayed. "I think I went into a kind of trance and then it seemed like the sound of their yelling and whooping was farther away." She could hear the horses' hooves in the distance, charging away down the road. She barely dared let out a sigh of relief. "I knew they might return after they had more liquor and got themselves all worked up," Grandmother remembered. "Sometimes, they went away first just as a warning, then they returned later to do their dirty deeds when they were drunk as fools."

After the men rode off and it was quiet for a long time, Cornelia climbed back into bed holding onto her husband's Civil War musket they kept hidden in the attic. But she couldn't sleep a wink and stared straight up at the ceiling, jumping at the first tiny sound she heard in the distance. Finally she could stand it no longer. She got up out of bed and put on her clothes. She packed a small satchel of food and ventured outside. She walked the back way from the cabin to the road that led to Durham. A sliver of moon was up, barely enough to guide her through the trees in the woods. She found the road and resolutely trudged the twelve miles to Durham rather than stay in that house alone.

She walked up to the little house that Grandfather rented and stood below the porch steps. She didn't want to wake the whole house. She went around to the back and rapped on the window where her husband slept. He saw her there, so tired and frightened, and came straight outside.

"What you doin' here, Miss Smith?" he respectfully asked her. "What the dickens happened to you?"

"Those Kluxers is riding out again. I couldn't stand it. They like to burn the house down with me inside it," Cornelia said, crossing her arms in defiance. "I rather walk these twelve miles in the dark than wait for that kind of dyin' all by myself out there. I ain't ready to meet my maker, not yet. They can have that old cabin."

But there was some truth to what those men had to say about Cornelia's parentage. She really was the daughter of Sidney Smith of Chapel Hill, North Carolina. Her mother, Harriet, was a woman who may not have had any African blood at all, but her body was owned by the Smiths. She was at least one-quarter Cherokee and a good part White.

Native American women were sometimes kidnapped and taken for brides by White settlers when White women were scarce in the territory. Their fair-skinned children were identified in the census as Colored, and were often sold into bondage for high prices.

Sidney Smith's father, Dr. James S. Smith, belonged to a prominent slave-holding family. He was a Democratic congressman who served one term from 1818 to 1820. When his two sons, Frank and Sidney, were away at the University of North Carolina studying medicine and law, and his remaining daughter, Mary, turned fifteen, he purchased Harriet for four hundred fifty dollars to be a companion and personal maid for Mary as she prepared to enter society as a young woman.

Before then, there were no people of mixed heritage on Dr. Smith's property. All his slaves were listed as Black in the census.

When Harriet was twenty, she asked Dr. Smith for permission to marry a free-born man named Reuben Day. Reuben's family had been free for generations, either by purchasing themselves or being emancipated by their White masters. Dr. Smith allowed the marriage, but they were not able to live together as husband and wife, and Reuben could only visit Harriet occasionally. Soon a son was born who, under the laws of the time, would be owned by the Smith family. Reuben vowed that one day he would buy his wife and son's freedom.

When the Smith brothers came home from college, they couldn't help noticing the beautiful young woman named Harriet who had become their sister's companion. Everyone admired Harriet's long straight black hair, her sharp features, and high cheekbones. When Frank and Sidney learned that Harriet was married to Reuben, they were irritated because they had their own plans for Harriet.

They waited for Reuben one night as he left Harriet's cabin. They dragged him to the back of the barn and beat him up so badly, he lay there a long time before he could raise himself up for the long walk home. The brothers threatened to kill him if he ever so much as set foot on the property. Harriet never saw her husband again, and he soon fled the county.

But trouble was brewing between the brothers. Frank warned Sidney to stay away from their sister's comely companion. But Sidney went after the vulnerable Harriet first. After visiting her in her cabin for some weeks, he forced himself upon her. Hearing her screams, Frank could stand it no longer. He waited for Sidney to come out and confronted him. Sidney was found lying unconscious in the yard the next morning. The family tried to cover it up by saying he'd had too much to drink the night before.

Both brothers left Harriet alone while she carried Sidney's child. When Cornelia was born, Sidney was so proud of being a father, he bragged to his buddies that he was the child's father. His sister

Mary did not feel comfortable with her niece being raised in the slave quarters, so she brought the baby girl into her house. She called in one of the women from the quarters to nurse and care for Cornelia. Harriet was not allowed to be a mother to her own daughter.

After the baby came, Frank decided it was his turn. He visited on a regular basis, and Harriet was thankful that at least she wasn't forced to be with the hated Sidney. She had three more girls with Frank, and each of them was taken from her to live in the big house with Mary Ruffin Smith. Miss Smith dressed them up every Sunday and took them to the Episcopal church where they had to sit by themselves up in the balcony. When people asked her about those pretty girls she brought to church, she just replied, "Those are my maid's daughters."

Cornelia later told her family, "We were free. We were just born into slavery, that's all."

Her father, Sidney, kept promising to leave his only daughter money in his will when he died, but somehow he never got around to it. After the war, Mary Smith offered her former slaves a place to farm rent free if they wished to stay, and most of them did, having nowhere else to go. Harriet's four daughters stayed with Miss Mary until they were married.

Pauli didn't like lying awake thinking about her grandmother's sad beginnings. At the first light coming in through the boxes piled against the windows, while Grandma was snoring as if she'd never wake up, Pauli quickly got out of bed and dressed. She pulled away the table with the chair on it and pried open the bedroom door. Careful not to knock over the oil lamp on the landing, she ran down the stairs, grabbed her books, and ran out of the house. There was only one place she could go so early in the morning.

She went to the house of Ruby and Ethel Green, two little girls whose parents had died. They lived with their older brother at the other end of Maplewood Cemetery. Pauli shivered as she walked along the cemetery fence to their house. Their brother was already gone from the house working in the tobacco factory where he rolled cigarettes to support them. They had to get themselves off to school each morning. The sisters left the back door open and kept the ladder up to their loft area where they slept. Pauli climbed up the ladder and slipped into the warmth of the covers between the two sisters to get another hour of sleep.

Pauli would walk to school with Ethel and Ruby, making sure to get there early because Aunt Pauline always wanted to see her before class to make sure she was dressed properly and to find out how the night went with Grandmother. Pauli usually finished up her homework then, which had been neglected from the night before.

One time, on their way to school, Ruby found a long rope.

"Look at this rope, how big it is," she said.

"We could use it for jump rope at recess. Won't the other girls be excited?" Pauli asked.

"Come on, you take one end and I'll take the other, Pauli. We'll carry it along with us to school."

They normally took a shortcut that went down a hill and across a small stream. When Pauli rushed to make her leap across the stream, the rope got tangled in her feet and she fell into the muddy bottom of the stream. Her pale blue dress, white shoes and socks got wet and stained with mud.

"What'll I do? If Aunt Pauline sees me like this, she'll ask how I messed up my clothes."

"I know what we can do," said Ruby, always ready with bright ideas. "We'll hurry on to school and you can wash your dress in the sink that's down there in the basement."

"And you can dry it on the warm radiators," chimed in Ethel after her sister.

"Well, let's hurry up then and forget about this old rope."

"No, we carried it all this way. We got to bring it in."

When Pauli appeared in front of Aunt Pauline, her dress was stiff from being dried on the radiator, and still showed the red mud from the stream.

"Now where have you been to get your dress stained so?" Aunt Pauline exclaimed.

"I was walking to school with Ethel and Ruby, and we found a rope and we were carrying it to school to play jump rope with."

"And where did you get so wet, might I ask?"

"We were jumping over that brook, over near Ethel and Ruby's house," Pauli blurted, the truth coming out almost against her will.

"And why were you coming to school from that way around? That's not how you usually go. Since when have you been walking to school with Ethel and Ruby?"

Pauli looked sheepishly at her shoes. "Since I been going to their house early in the morning to get some sleep because Grandma keeps me awake all night with her prowling around and shouting at the intruders."

"Oh, my Lord, you've been going over to the Green children's house to sleep?"

"Yes, ma'am."

"Well, I'll be, child. I just don't know. Maybe it's time for me to come home."

Chapter 8

Education

Pauli's family had settled in Durham Station when it was just a stop on the train between Greensboro and Raleigh. Her Fitzgerald cousins settled a few miles from the center of Durham on the western edge of town so they could be near the clay deposits that supplied their brick factory. Pauli's great uncle, Richard Fitzgerald, became one of the wealthiest men in Durham. He had an entrepreneurial spirit that his brother Robert lacked, and he wasn't held back by the vision problems that plagued Robert. He was able to leverage his brick business into other areas and owned many properties he rented out. His family actually lived in an eighteen-room house in a White neighborhood.

Pauli asked her favorite cousin how they were able to live in that part of town.

"Don't you know the story?" her cousin answered. "There was a White man who had a grudge against his neighbor because of some business deal that didn't come out right. This man went and sold his own house to Daddy just so he could have revenge on neighbor. How do you like that?" she added proudly.

Most of the more well-off Black families settled closer to the center of town in a section of Durham called Hayti. To get to her high school, Pauli had to walk three miles. When she was on the basketball team, it was difficult for her to get back from the night games and parties that sometimes went on after games. One day she complained to Aunt Pauline.

"I wished we lived in town like the rich children in Hayti."

Aunt Pauline was standing at the kitchen table cutting up a chicken, with a knife in one hand and the leg of the chicken in the other. When she heard Pauli's complaint, her arms froze in midair. She laid the chicken down and placed the knife flat on the table. She said quietly, "Don't ever let me hear you talking about 'rich children in Hayti' again, Miss Pauli. Your family stands with the best. It's not what you have, but who you *are* that counts."

"I'm sorry, Aunt Pauline," Pauli murmured. "I just wish I were closer to school, that's all."

The social life in high school was in Hayti, and Pauli was eager to participate. She decided she needed a bicycle, so she began saving the money she earned from odd jobs and errands she managed to do before and after school. She saved money from her Saturday morning paper route that she'd kept up since she was ten. She even saved the change Aunt Pauline gave her for the streetcar when it was cold and rainy. She always put that money in her pocket and trudged through the rain to school.

All her chores didn't stop Pauli from keeping up with her studies. The only area where she came up short sometimes was in conduct. She had the most trouble with her English teacher, Mrs. Louise Whitted Burton, who was from one of the prominent families who lived in Hayti. Her father was Durham's first African American postman. Mrs. Burton was one of the oldest teachers in the school and a very strict disciplinarian.

One day in May of Pauli's senior year, when the weather was getting hot and the students could barely stand to be indoors, a boy named Edwin started throwing erasers around the classroom and one of them struck the side of Pauli's head. Before she had time to think about it, Pauli scooped the eraser off the floor and raised her arm to hurl it back at the boy—just as Mrs. Burton stepped into the room. Old Mrs. Burton stopped at the door and called out in her shrill voice, "Miss Murray, don't even think of throwing that eraser. Step over to my desk immediately."

Pauli's arm came down and she walked sheepishly to Mrs. Burton's desk.

"Miss Murray, I am afraid I am going to have to report this to your homeroom teacher. I'll make sure she gives you a C in conduct this semester."

Pauli knew this would mean she wouldn't be awarded the Certificate of Distinction at the commencement ceremonies in June. She assumed she must have a perfect record to win the award. Pauli knew she had straight As in all her classes, and was mortified that she would have a glaring C in conduct.

Pauli became so demoralized that when graduation came, she sat

Graduation from Richmond Hill High School, New York City, 1927.

in the back of the gym away from the senior class. When the principal called out her name, she was caught off guard. She stayed where she was because she thought it was a mistake. But the students around her encouraged her to go on up, and everyone turned their heads, staring at her expectantly. So she got up and made her way alone across the old wooden floorboards of the gym up to the stage.

The principal gave her a big smile and shook her hand as he handed her the coveted certificate. Pauli supposed her homeroom teacher had put her on the list regardless of her shameful C in conduct. But, as she turned to make her way down the steps from the stage, she saw the menacing Mrs. Burton bustling her way down the aisle, coming straight toward her with a fearsome look on her face. She met Pauli at the bottom step and snatched the certificate right out of her hands.

"I am sorry, Mr. Principal," Mrs. Burton intoned so the whole hall could hear, "there has been a mistake. Miss Murray doesn't have a perfect record. She received a C in conduct this spring. It would be unfair to the students with no such blemish on their records were she to receive this award." The principal was too stunned to contradict her. Pauli could do nothing but walk the long way back down the center aisle as humiliated as she ever hoped to be in life. Yet this wouldn't be the last time a deserved award or position would be taken away from her.

Pauli was only ten when she finished the sixth grade. And she graduated at the top of her class in high school when she was only fifteen. She participated in all the extracurricular activities she could and was the leader in most of them. She especially liked playing forward on the girls' basketball team. Their coach was the best basketball player at the school and he let them play by boys' rules, using the entire court instead of only half. Pauli was editor-in-chief of the school newspaper, president of the literary society, and secretary of her class, as well as a member of the debating team.

Her graduation picture shows a young lady in a white dress with short bobbed hair in the new style of the 1920s. She looks feminine, but the page shows her name as "Paul." Some of her girlfriends also had boyish nicknames like "Jack" or "Sam." For Pauli it was the first of many masculine names she gave herself. Among her friends, she sometimes called herself "Pete," or referred to herself as "Pixie," or "the Dude."

Pauli received a scholarship to attend Wilberforce University in Ohio, but the scholarship was only for one semester and didn't pay for room and meals, so she had to turn it down. Her only alternative was North Carolina College for Negroes in Durham. But Pauli was determined not to attend a segregated college. In fact, she didn't want to go to a Southern college at all; she wanted to go to school in the North. Ever since she saw the sweater her favorite teacher at Hillside High wore—a sporty red sweater with a big white C emblazoned on it. Pauli had asked the teacher what school it stood for.

"Why, that stands for Columbia, Pauli. I was lucky enough to take some summer classes there."

Pauli didn't realize she had meant Columbia Teachers College. She thought she was referring to Columbia University in New York. Teachers College was part of Columbia, but it was a graduate school. Pauli held the secret hope that she could one day be enrolled at Columbia. When she told Aunt Pauline she wanted to go to college in New York, Pauline said she would put her mind on it and write Cousin Maude to see if they could stay with her while they looked into it.

The Reverend Eugene Henderson and his wife Lula offered to drive them north. They had no children and enjoyed taking long road trips. They traveled in the reverend's 1925 Ford roadster on US Route 1, at the time a gravelly dirt road that occasionally turned into asphalt. They drove the car onto a ferry to get from New Jersey to Manhattan.

Pauli was entranced by the big metropolis of New York. She loved everything about it. She wrote her Aunt Sallie back home:

> *I love the skyscrapers, the Statue of Liberty, the amusements at Coney Island, the double-decker buses on Fifth Avenue, and the theaters on Broadway (we didn't go inside, of course). And, Aunt Sallie, at a restaurant called the Automat, you can put your nickels in a slot and out come dishes of hot food! What I love best about New York*

is that we may sit anywhere we choose in the subway
trains, on the buses, and on the streetcars. And at the
movies, there is no special section for Colored. Someday
I'm going to live in New York City.

Cousin Maude was Grandfather Fitzgerald's niece, the daughter of his sister Agnes, whom Pauli's mother was named after. Maude and her husband lived in a two-story brick house with their three sons in the Richmond Hill section of Queens. All of the identical houses on the street were built during the boom time of the 1920s. As Maude pointed out the neighbors on the street, Pauli observed, "They have such strange sounding names."

"Most of these houses are owned by European immigrants, Pauli. They're Irish, German, Italian, Polish, and Armenian. There are only two other Colored families in Richmond Hill. We don't like to make too much of it," she added.

Pauli did not realize until much later that her cousin Maude and her family had maintained a quiet charade in not advertising their background. Most people thought they were White with their olive complexions and soft brown hair. Still, they opened their home to Pauli whose darker complexion must have been a curiosity to the neighbors.

Pauli insisted they visit Columbia University first. It was a few stops down from 125th Street on the subway on the West Side. The lady at the admissions office told them Columbia didn't admit women, and she referred them to Barnard College for Women across the street.

At Barnard, they sat in plush red leather chairs in the somber office decorated with oriental rugs and paintings of distinguished professors on the dark mahogany walls.

"You must know that this is a private institution," the admissions counselor said, looking directly over her spectacles at Pauline. "It requires a good deal of money to go to Barnard. And our students on scholarship are very highly qualified." She looked carefully over Pauli's transcript from Hillside High.

"Mrs. Dame, although your Pauli seems to have done quite well judging by her grades, I'm afraid the secondary institution she attended has not given her the rigorous training required of our young women. A good grounding in many subject areas is totally missing here—Latin, French, advanced mathematics, and the sciences." She stopped mid-sentence as if nothing more need be said.

Pauli hung her head, trying to hold back her tears, swallowing the disappointment, frustration, anger and shame that her people had not been given the opportunity to achieve to the same level as others. The woman must have seen her dejected demeanor as they stood up to leave. As they were going out the door, she called them back.

"Mrs. Dame, why don't you try Hunter College? It's a public college. Anyone who is a resident of New York and passes the entrance exams may attend without paying tuition. You might want to visit them. I'll give you directions."

As they rode on the bus to Park Avenue and 68th Street, Pauli bristled with her characteristic stubbornness.

"If I am not going to go to a segregated college, I don't see why I have to go to a college that only admits women. It's against my principles."

"Darling, let's see whether you have the qualifications to get into the institution first, before we snub our noses at it. Remember, the high school system in Durham that you went to only went up to the eleventh grade."

The admissions officer at Hunter was friendly but firm, repeating the concerns of the admissions officer at Barnard. "I'm afraid, Miss Murray, you are missing more than a year of the high school credits needed to qualify for admission. You need another year of English, French, and Latin, as well as biology, chemistry, and trigonometry. It looks to me like it would take another year and a half to two years to complete these courses. However, if you took them in a New York City high school and received a diploma, that would make you automatically eligible to attend Hunter."

The two women made their way back to Queens and told Cousin Maude the situation. Maude sat at the kitchen table and said, "Well, I suppose you could enroll at Richmond Hill High School here in Queens and start your courses. But I don't know if we could keep you for more than a school year."

"Cousin Maude, if you would let me stay with you for one year, I know I could finish those requirements," Pauli entreated. "I would put my whole heart and soul into it."

"But what about the residency requirements?" Aunt Pauline interjected. "You have to establish legal residency, and with no legal guardians, how would we do that?"

That's when Uncle James spoke up, even though he was hard of hearing. "Why, we'll just have to get letters of adoption, if that's what it takes. I've heard of people doing that before."

Next they went to the principal's office at Richmond Hill. With Aunt Pauline's gentle persuasion and her credentials as a teacher, the principal allowed Pauli to enroll as a senior. She was given full credit for all the subjects she had taken at Hillside in Durham.

"But you will have to take certain statewide Regents Examinations in order to receive a diploma," the principal warned. "The total number of subjects you will need to take are more than what a single student is allowed during a school year. I am going to turn you over to an advisor who will see that you are allowed to sit in on the extra classes without being formally enrolled. If, at the end of the year, you pass the Regents Exams in these subjects with a grade of at least seventy-five, you will receive full class credit for them."

Aunt Pauline couldn't help sighing, a little worried about all that her precious namesake would be undertaking. Finally, she turned to her adopted child and said, "Well, I guess the rest is up to you, Miss Pauline."

Pauli hadn't wanted to be at a segregated school. At Richmond Hill, she found she was the only Black student among four thousand!

"Well," she laughed, "I don't have to worry that social concerns might distract me from my work!"

The students regarded her with curiosity and laughed at her Southern accent, but their interest was friendly. Still, Pauli could not throw off the anxiety she felt about competing with White students her age. More than anything, if she came up short she didn't want it to be attributed to racial inferiority.

She was shocked to receive her first grades—a sixty-five in Latin and seventy-seven in French. This for a girl who had been voted "most studious" in her senior class and had graduated with top honors. She found she performed best in physics and American history, two courses that did not require previous knowledge.

But those initial middling grades only spurred her determination. She studied far into the night and often fell asleep over her books.

She was no help to Cousin Maude, who had harbored a vain hope that Pauli would be of some use in the household with her three boys. But Pauli was hopeless at housekeeping. She wouldn't even hang up her own clothes or keep her dresser drawers in order. While Cousin Maude continually swept and dusted and polished the floors till they gleamed, Pauli was totally oblivious to her surroundings.

Pauli graduated with her class, but she still had to earn enough money for her room and board before she could enroll at Hunter. She made the trip back to Durham for the summer and got a job as a junior stenographer doing filing for the Bankers Fire Insurance Company. She worked with ten people all in one big room, each at their own desk. Her supervisor, Miss Felicia Miller, taught her how to use the mimeograph machine and other office equipment. Pauli chafed under the woman's strict direction, and complained to her aunts. "Miss Miller seldom hands out compliments and she rides me unmercifully if I make mistakes." But when Pauli was ready to leave for college, Miss Miller arranged for Pauli to receive a retroactive raise in one lump sum to help her get started with her studies.

Before leaving Durham, Pauli went to pay her respects to the Episcopalian bishop of their diocese. Bishop Delaney was confined to his bed with a terminal illness, but his eyes showed delight as Mrs. Dame and her daughter came to his bedside. They talked about Pauli's future and then prayed together. After the prayers, Bishop Delaney took Pauli's hand and said, "You are a child of destiny, my dear." In later years, Aunt Pauline wouldn't let her forget those words.

"Remember, you have been blessed by a bishop on his deathbed. That means something and you must live up to his words, Pauli."

Pauli thought of those words many times in her life when she was up against a difficult trial as she blazed new trails in spite of the many obstacles that lay in her path.

Chapter 9

On Her Own

It was 1928, a year before the Great Crash of the stock market. Pauli returned to New York to live with her cousin Maude and began her freshman year at Hunter College in Brooklyn. She joined girls from all over Brooklyn and Queens who converged on the elevated subway, the Fulton Street El. The girls ran through the cars, shrieking and giggling, full of excitement after their classes let out. But by the time the train pulled into her station in Queens, Pauli was the only one left. All her friends lived far away, so she did most of her visiting with them during these rides to and from school.

Pauli made two friends who would be dear to her throughout her life. Out of five thousand students at Hunter, only one hundred were African American. One of them was the only other woman of color in Pauli's freshman class at the Brooklyn Annex. Her name was Lula Burton, and she eventually became the principal of a junior high school in New York. Pauli was grateful to have someone like herself to confide in. She harbored a sense of inferiority about her skills and knowledge compared to the White students in her classes. Perhaps it was because her Southern accent seemed to set her apart. She didn't know if some of her academic stumbling was just because her school hadn't been able to prepare her or if she was just a little slow in mastering the subjects. She was curious to know how Lula handled herself.

Lula was tall and slender and carried herself in a regal manner. She had lovely olive skin and large hazel eyes that were not ashamed to look straight into another person's gaze. Her voice was musical with a deep resonance and the natural rhythm of her speech was like poetry. Pauli loved to listen to her and was always glad to hear her speak in class. She not only carried herself well in responding to teachers, but she also had a way of speaking to the White students that was friendly and confident. Pauli was able to learn from her that relations with the other students did not have to be so strained. She had a natural gift for languages, a skill Pauli struggled to master.

When Pauli visited Lula's brownstone on Decatur Street, they would sit on the front steps and Lula would read aloud the great poets of the day: Carl Sandburg and Robert Frost, Sara Teasdale and Edna St. Vincent Millay. She also read the great Black poets just beginning to be published—Claude McKay, Countee Cullen, and Langston Hughes—taking Pauli far beyond the boundaries of Laurence Dunbar, whom Pauli had learned about in school.

Pauli loved to write and her mind seemed about to burst with all the things she wanted to say, but she had much to learn about grammar and using imagery to get her ideas across. Her class essays came back consistently marked with C-minuses and even Ds. Finally she wrote an essay about her Grandfather Fitzgerald and his time fighting in the Union Army during the Civil War. Perhaps because she remembered his stories so vividly and wrote about them with such love for her grandfather, this essay came back with an A-minus. She did not know then that it would be the starting point for the book *Proud Shoes* she would one day write, the story of her family of proud and determined Americans.

Pauli's other good friend was Pauline Diner, a German-Jewish girl with gentle dark eyes that revealed her great sympathy and generosity toward others. She was in Pauli's German class, which was filled with

Jewish girls who already spoke German or Yiddish in their homes. Their participation made the class go that much faster. Pauli could barely keep up. When Pauline saw what a hard time Pauli was having, she offered to coach her while they rode together on the Brooklyn train.

Not only did they study during their regular train time, they would arrange to meet on the train an hour early. Using the time to study, they sat on a bench on the platform reciting the declensions above the din of the subway trains traveling back and forth on their rusty tracks. Even with all that help, Pauli barely made it through the class with a D, but she might not have passed at all if it hadn't been for the caring concern of her friend. Pauline even invited Pauli for her family's Friday night prayers and to some religious holidays, such as Passover and Rosh Hashanah.

During her time with cousin Maude, Pauli had her first experience in an Episcopal Church with more elaborate "high church" rituals than her family's church at home. The Fitzgeralds had, of course, never been to the Episcopal church that served the Whites in Durham. Pauli remembered her grandmother's stories of having to sit with her sisters high above the sanctuary in the balcony where the Black parishoners were forced to sit. They were not allowed to come into the main sanctuary to take Communion with the rest of the parishioners.

At first Pauli was put off by all the pageantry of the Anglican liturgy at her cousin's church. There was a good deal of chanting and the priest, who wore elaborate white robes with golden vestments, swung burning incense while bells rang out during the service. Pauli didn't know what any of it meant, but she felt at peace being a part of it and she would find solace in this liturgy later in life.

Still, life with Cousin Maude was lonely for Pauli. She had no friends nearby, so she jumped at the chance when another cousin invited her to work at the West 137th Street YWCA in Harlem. Susie Elliot, who had a degree from the Pratt Institute in New York, had become the house director there after having taught home economics at the Y for a number of years. Pauli would cross paths with her again when Elliot became the dean of women at Howard University. One night a week, Pauli filled in for the switchboard operator and the elevator girl. She worked from five until midnight, then she would sleep at Susie's and go to school the next morning on the train. Pauli was so happy there, she moved into the Y a few weeks later and started living on her own for the first time in her life.

To pay for her room and board, she worked afternoons and evenings as a dishwasher and steam table runner in the Y cafeteria. Cousin Maude did not make much of an effort to get her to stay in Queens. In fact, having the dark-skinned girl in her household had upset the delicate balance in her community she tried to maintain by presenting herself as a person of European immigrant origins.

Pauli loved living on her own. Her room on the fourth floor was special to her because it faced the back of the Abyssinian Baptist Church. This church, with its ebullient choir and lively organ music, was entirely different from her Episcopal church at home. Pauli continued to attend an Episcopal church, St. Philip's Episcopal on West 134ᵗʰ Street, but during the choir rehearsals at Abyssinian, Pauli had to stop whatever she was doing in her room just to listen to their joyful noise. The assistant minister there was Adam Clayton Powell Jr., who would later become Harlem's representative in the United States Congress.

For the rest of the term, Pauli commuted to Brooklyn. When summer came, she was happy to have a job and the whole summer off from school. She borrowed a bicycle from the recreation director at the Y and toured up and down the island of Manhattan. She wrote her aunts down in Durham:

> I ride all over Manhattan—up to the Cloisters, down Riverside Drive along the Hudson River, through Central Park, down Fifth Avenue past all the shops where rich people go, and down to Washington Square and

Greenwich Village—and then to Battery Park and South Ferry, and along Delancey and Orchard Streets on the Lower East Side. So far, I have gotten knocked off my bike in traffic five times, but miraculously I have escaped serious injury, and best of all, my borrowed bicycle has not suffered any wounds.

One evening when Pauli was working the elevator at the Y, an attractive woman in her early thirties boarded the elevator. Before getting off, she handed Pauli a small embroidered silk case. Inside the case was a black pocket-sized comb with a Japanese floral design painted on the bridge.

"I'd like to offer you a little present," the woman said. "You see, I just lost my temper downstairs, and whenever I lose my temper I must do penance," she explained. "I must give someone something that I cherish very much. I know you are a worthy person and I want to give this to you." When they came to bottom floor, she exited the elevator and disappeared.

Pauli wondered, who was this mysterious woman? She asked the receptionist downstairs.

"Oh, that's Juliette Derricotte," the receptionist replied. "She's the national student secretary for the YWCA. She used to be a delegate to the convention of the World's Student Christian Federation."

Pauli tried to meet her again, but heard she'd taken a position as dean of women at Fisk University in Tennessee. Pauli never forgot that gesture of kindness from a stranger. But her memory of the generous woman was overshadowed by the knowledge that, two years later, Miss Derricotte was in an automobile accident while traveling in the South. She died while being transported to a hospital many miles away because the nearest hospital for Whites Only refused to give her emergency treatment.

While Pauli was a sophomore at Hunter College she worked a five-hour shift as a dinner waitress at Firenze, a restaurant that was part of a chain owned by Alice Foote MacDougall. When Pauli came in at 5 p.m., she walked past the White hostesses and White cashiers who were eating their restaurant meals on white linens in the dining room. Pauli tried not to look at them as she crossed the room and went down the stairs to the basement where the Black employees, the cooks and the waitresses and the dishwashers, were all seated at bare wooden tables. She hung up her worn coat and sat down next to her friend Ellie.

"Sit down, child, if you're hungry, but don't expect much. These leftovers are so tasteless, I like to throw them into the trash," Ellie complained. Then she brightened with an idea. "Pauli, will you try to order an extra lasagne dinner tonight? I'll grab it off your tray when you're taking it from the kitchen. I'll give you half." Pauli hadn't tried that ruse yet, but she was tempted that night. She hadn't eaten lunch in order to save money for the train fare home.

At that time in New York, even though public facilities were legally integrated, many restaurants still refused to serve African Americans. People from out of town didn't always know that the law was not enforced. Tonight, Pauli looked up from wrapping the silverware in napkins and watched as an elderly, well-dressed Black couple entered the restaurant. They stood quietly next to the entrance waiting to be recognized. It took the hostess a long time to get back to her station. She was a young girl who was usually very pleasant to all the staff, but she kept making excuses to avoid approaching the couple, arranging salt shakers on the tray and going to tables asking patrons if they needed anything.

"She's just hoping they will clear outta here," whispered Ellie as she brushed past Pauli on her way to the kitchen. But the couple just stood there expectantly. Pauli and the other waitresses kept glancing over at them in sympathy. Ellie got word back to the kitchen and George the cook opened the swinging door and stood there watching with the dishwashers standing behind him. Finally, the hostess went back to her place and just stared uncomfortably at the dignified couple.

"We'd like a table for two, ma'am," the gentleman prodded her.

"I'm sorry," the girl muttered almost inaudibly, "it is the policy of this restaurant not to serve Negroes. Perhaps there is another establishment down the street you could go to." She looked around nervously. By now all the servers had stopped performing their tasks to watch the scene, and not a few of the patrons were looking up from their meals.

Ellie whispered to Pauli, "I swear, if she don't let them two sit down, I'm going to quit this job."

"You can't do that, Ellie. But maybe we could protest in some other way." As Pauli put her head to a strategy, George started taking off his apron. He spoke in an even voice, loud enough so the hostess and just about everyone in the restaurant could hear.

"I don't know what's come over me, but I suddenly feel under the weather like. I think I'm gonna have to go home."

One of the dishwashers joined him. "You know, I think I got the same bug, too. It must be catching."

Then Ellie chimed in: "I do declare, it's downright infectious, whatever it is. I'm feeling rather poorly myself. Aren't you feeling just a little bit faint, Pauli?"

Pauli saw that a protest could be spontaneous, and she quickly joined in. "Yes, Ellie, a certain fatigue has come over me. I am downright sick and tired."

Without any kind of organizing, the Black staff stopped what they were doing, went to the backroom, got their coats, and filed out of that restaurant while the diners and White employees looked on with dismay. Even though the restaurant didn't change its policy, Pauli saw that good people could join together to stand up for what they believed was right. It was her first experience protesting the indignities of segregation. She would continue to be involved in a number of protests in the 1930s and '40s, many years before a woman named

Rosa Parks refused to sit in the back of a city bus in Montgomery, Alabama, in 1955.

Life during her college years wasn't all work and no play. Pauli liked to get out of the city when she could, and often hitchhiked with friends to save money. In March of 1931, Pauli and her friend Dorothy Hayden, whom she affectionately nicknamed "Toni," hitchhiked to Newport, Rhode Island, where Toni's family lived. For safety, they wore Boy Scout uniforms and practiced speaking in a low register as they bantered back and forth like regular chums.

After an uneventful ride with a traveling salesman, they were let off at the train station in Bridgeport, Connecticut, where they planned to use the restrooms. At that time, members of the Traveler's Aid Society might be strolling through the station to help stranded travelers, but they also kept an eye out for vagrants or people engaging in questionable activity. That afternoon, one of them saw a young Boy Scout enter the women's bathroom. When Toni walked out, the Traveler's Aid officer confronted her.

"Young man, may I ask why you are coming out of the ladies' room?"

"Me?" Toni looked around in amusement. "Why, it could be because I'm a girl, and I have every right to use the ladies' room."

"But you're dressed like a Boy Scout!" the woman insisted.

"Oh, you mean this?" Toni looked down at her khaki pants and waved her olive-green necktie. "I always wear a Boy Scout uniform when I travel." She leaned forward and whispered conspiratorially, "Keeps the young men away from me, you know?"

The woman continued to press her. "Are you traveling alone?"

"Well," Toni began, but then the woman's gaze rested on the door of the men's room, from which a second Boy Scout emerged.

"I see you are not alone," the woman uttered in horror. She now thought she was confronting two underage lovers on their way to elopement—or worse. She immediately called a policeman over.

Pauli realized she would have to confess. "Officer—ma'am," she added respectfully, tipping her Scout hat unconsciously. "We weren't trying to fool anyone. We were only having some fun. We're just a couple of girls working on an article for our college newspaper."

They ended up spending the night at the Bridgeport Protective Home, arranged by the Traveler's Aid officer. In the morning they had a hearty breakfast of pancakes and bacon and proceeded on their way.

Pauli kept a scrapbook of her road trips, which she titled, *Vagabondia*. Their escapade was written up in the Bridgeport newspaper, the story headlined, "Slip Brings Halt to Tour of Two Girls." In her scrapbook, next to the news item, Pauli pasted another story about a girl who always dressed like a boy, whose mother did not discourage her. Pauli must have been reminded of her aunt who had indulged her childhood desire to wear boys' clothes as well. To prove the point, she pasted a photo of herself sitting on a ledge in sporty white slacks with turned up cuffs, holding a white fedora hat. She titled the photo: "The Dude, 1931."

Pauli Murray in white outfit, calling herself, "The Dude," 1931.

Chapter 10

Riding the Rails

In the summer of 1929, when Pauli started working at the Firenze restaurant in the theater district, its customers were people who wanted to get a bite to eat after seeing a show. People waited in line to get a table and Pauli made good tips off the generous customers. The crash of the stock market in October changed all of that. The clientele dwindled and some nights Pauli didn't even make enough for carfare home. She had to walk to the restaurant from school and eat her first meal of the day there. It was Pauli's second year at Hunter and she'd lost fifteen pounds. Eating pilfered appetizers at the restaurant was not enough to sustain her.

When the restaurant let her go, she joined the thousands of men and women who were looking for work. She tried a job as a housekeeper for a woman in Greenwich Village, but was fired after attempting to cook a meal. She answered an unusual ad for "an intelligent Colored girl" in a White-owned travel agency. Having tamed her Southern accent by then, she passed the audition for her telephone voice. She got the job, but when the company merged with a group arranging tours to Russia, her position was eliminated. Even so, this job would come to haunt her in later years because of its association with the Soviet Union and its communist government.

Looking for her luck to change, Pauli helped a friend drive west three thousand miles on Route 30, all the way to California. They drove through the endless flatness of wheat fields in Nebraska and climbed the curving highways of the Rocky Mountains where they took in the wide, sweeping views. They idled with a long line of cars as huge flocks of sheep crossed the tarred road as they were driven to their spring feeding grounds. She put her reflections in a poem called "Song of the Highway," which was published in 1970 in her book of poetry, *Dark Testament*.

But her carefree independence was not to last. When she arrived in Vallejo, California, she was greeted with troubling news. A letter from Aunt Pauline indicated that she was ill and she asked Pauli to come stay with her now that she was out of school. She had not known that Pauli was touring the country. Pauli had to send a telegram that she had no fare to return, and her aunt wired back saying she didn't have the money to send her. She added ruefully, "You'll have to get yourself out of your own predicaments, I'm afraid."

Pauli never doubted that she must return home to help care for her surrogate parent. She considered hitchhiking back, but the long stretches of empty highway she'd driven through on her way out West and the dangers of traveling alone made her reconsider. Her hosts told her that folks were riding the freight trains to make the trip back East. They said you could do it in two weeks. Pauli decided to give it a try.

It was 1931 and more than two hundred thousand homeless young people were using the freight cars to travel around in their search for jobs across the country. They congregated in hobo "jungles" near the railroad tracks. The Children's Bureau of the US Department of Labor labeled their movement a "tragic army." Teenagers were just a small part of the three million homeless men and women traveling the country in search of work.

Pauli was still underweight and, at five feet tall, was often mistaken for an adolescent. She had no trouble dressing like a boy, as she always wore slacks when she wasn't working. She still purchased casual, outdoor clothes from the boys' section of department stores. To prepare for her journey, she put on khaki pants, a blue work shirt, a sturdy pair of shoes, and her brown leather jacket. In a small knapsack she carried a tin cup, a plate, and a few utensils. Her hair was cropped in a boyish cut. If she kept her voice low, she could easily be mistaken for one of the many desperate young men who became hobos during the Great Depression. Her friends drove her to the Oakland trainyard where the Southern Pacific Railroad cars were resting on the tracks like slumbering elephants waiting for their journey eastward.

"We'll wait here to make sure you get safely aboard one of these freight cars," one of her friends said.

"No, you better not," Pauli said. "I think I need to make my own way. You'll cause more attention from the guards. You better go."

Pauli walked up to a group of young boys, about sixteen or seventeen years old, thinking they would accept her more readily as one of them. In a clearing within a clump of bushes not far from the tracks, they were warming their hands over a barrel of burning rolled newspapers and old pieces of cardboard they had dragged from empty fruit boxes pilfered from the yard. In the clearing there were crates and boxes to sit on and a few tattered mattresses flung about for troubled sleep.

One of the boys spoke up, brushing away the blonde hair falling over his eyes as he suspiciously regarded this stranger with tawny skin. "What are you?"

"Look like he Colored, dat's all," said one of their comrades. "You know we all mixed-up in this ol' US of A."

Pauli shrugged off their banter, relieved that she'd passed the test of not being taken for a girl.

"You new at this?" another boy asked. "You look as green as a sour apple. Your clothes ain't even dirty."

"I drove a beat up ol' Chevy out here with a buddy, but I got to get back home on account of my ma is sick and I gotta help her out," Pauli answered, trying to give herself an air of bravado. "I never rode the rails before. Folks say hitchin' a ride on a locomotive is the fastest way to get to where you're goin'.'"

"It may be fast, but it's a heap more dangerous," the boy warned.

"It ain't so bad if you know the ropes," his buddy piped up.

"What do you have to do to get on one of these cars?" Pauli asked.

"Well, first you gotta stay away from them railroad bulls. Them hired guards that run along the top of the cars while the old iron horse is pickin' up speed, why, they carry guns and they'll use em."

"They shoot to kill?"

"I don't know if they *aimin'* to kill, but it ain't like they'd care if they did, seein' as how we're *trespassin'* on private property. I know a guy got shot in the leg by one of those bulls, and he's limpin' on his leg still. Can't run fast enough now to hop the freight no more."

"What's the other way?"

"You have to wait till those bulls climb down off the trains. The owners don't want to pay them to ride the whole way. They get off just before the train gets out of the yard. That's when you want to make your jump. You gotta run fast to catch on. Otherwise, you could be thrown under the wheels as you're swingin' yourself up."

Finally, Pauli could listen no more to their dire warnings. "Is any of you gonna climb aboard one of these locomotives or are you all gonna just stand here and talk about it?"

"Hold on now, Greenie. You gotta pick your transport. We's all waitin' for the proper ride. Can't just ride any ol' car. Out of Oakland here, you kin ride a fruit train or a butter'n'egg train. Me, I'm waitin' for a 'hot shot.' Them's the faster express freights. They don't stop at every hodunk town where you have a chance of meetin' up with more bulls. Joe here's waitin' on a 'manifesto.' It goes nonstop all the way to Chicago."

"I go for the 'reefer' cars when they're carryin' oranges," a slight White boy about the same size as Pauli piped up. "They got a ice chest at the end of every car but they leave 'em empty when they're carryin' oranges. You kin get in one of those and ride sweet all the way. One a them'll be going out this evening around ten o'clock. We seen 'em loading it up this afternoon."

"I'll go with you," Pauli said, realizing that 'reefer' meant refrigerator, not the rolled-up cigarettes whose sweet smell she remembered from the streets of Harlem. "What's your name?"

"They call me Oklahoma, on account o' where I'm from. What about you?"

"My name's Pete. I'm from North Carolina."

"Welcome aboard," Oklahoma smiled. "You and me'll make a good team, being on the small side, the better to crawl through tight spaces." The boys sat around listening to stories until the sun started to set, then they edged their way around the perimeter of the yard, waiting for cover of dark. They could see the men finishing up loading the big crates of oranges.

"I know a place to hide while the bulls are parading around. After they get off, the train picks up speed fast, 'cause it's an express. I don't want to risk not catchin' it."

Pauli "catching the old freight."

When the bulls on top of the car paced in the other direction, Pauli and Oklahoma made their move. One of their buddies on the ground threw rocks to divert the bulls' attention. They climbed up between the cars and flattened their small frames in the crevice, where they couldn't be seen from above.

After the train started rumbling and snorting, and they heard the receding footsteps of the guards, they climbed into the car and spied the empty ice chest with a trapdoor at the top held open by a jack. There was just enough room to squeeze through to get inside. The walls were made of steel plates and the floor was made of wooden slats. The crates of oranges were stacked below the floor, emanating a faint citrusy smell.

They waited anxiously, hearing the switch engine shunting the car back and forth. They heard the clanging of the red and green signal lanterns readying the train to pull out. Finally, the whistle blew in a great burst of exploding steam. Rattling and complaining, the iron horse creaked and groaned, shivered and shook, and finally pulled its weight out of the yard.

As they settled in for the long haul, Oklahoma looked around in the minimal light that came through the opening, and mused, "If that steel jack collapses, we're goners. We'd be sealed inside and no one would know we're here. I don't even know if they could hear us yelling." He added ruefully, "I don't believe we'd last too long." Pauli kept her silent prayers to herself.

The two stowaways hugged their own bodies for warmth and slept till hunger awoke them before dawn.

"How long do you think this ride is gonna be?" Pauli asked. "We don't have any food or water."

"I'm hopin' this baby is goin' across the Rockies. Could be another twelve to fourteen hours. Mebbe we kin find a way to get to them oranges. I kin smell 'em from here and it's makin' me hungry."

The scruffy boy and girl passed their hands over every inch of the cell along the floorboards. Finally, they loosened the wooden slats. They worked their fingers underneath the partition and got through to the crates. Oklahoma managed to tear open the edge of a crate, with his knife as a lever. Pauli reached her hand in, bruising and scratching her fingers against the rough wood, until she felt the crinkly tissue paper that encircled the precious cargo. When they'd amassed almost thirty of the fresh round globes, they peeled and quartered them and voraciously ate them all on the spot. Afterward, they wrapped the peelings in the purple tissue paper and tossed them out the trapdoor to hide any trace of their theft.

The express came to a halt on one of the hundreds of tracks in the Chicago train yard. Pauli and Oklahoma hoisted themselves up, slid through the opening in the ice chest, and scrambled out of the reefer, ducking behind cars and venturing out into the Windy City to find food. They were told to look for Sally's—the Salvation Army—it had the heartiest soup.

They caught a ride out of Chicago in a cattle car carrying a load of wooden boxes. They made a seat at the top of the boxes and rode there for the next eight hours.

They climbed down off the train in Sandusky, Ohio, and encountered a hobo jungle located beside a pretty stream. Fireflies joined in with the sparks from the blazing campfire. The stew pot was on; water from the brook was boiling. The hobos began to empty their pockets in preparation for mulligan stew. One hobo had an onion he'd pinched from a fruit market, another had several potatoes and an ear of corn taken from a farmer's field, another took out a handful of navy beans he'd carried in his pocket for days, others gathered dandelions and wild leeks and contributed them to the stew. Anything edible was cast into the pot, along with bits of Bull Durham tobacco and pocket lint.

Pauli dipped into the pot with her tin cup and ate heartily, sitting with the men and listening as they swapped tall tales of the road. Many talked of home and loved ones and the positions they'd held before their worlds collapsed.

Oklahoma couldn't bear to leave this idyllic spot just yet, so they parted ways. Pauli caught a train alone and spent the night inside another open reefer. A strange silence woke her the next morning after the engines cut off when the train slid into Philadelphia. She climbed out of the car right into the arms of a yard policeman strolling up and down the platform.

"Now, what are you doin' in there, boy?" the officer said with a degree of sympathy in his voice.

"I'm not a boy, officer," Pauli suddenly blurted, too weary to continue her charade. "I'm a college student trying to get home to take care of my aunt who wired me that she was sick in Durham. I drove with a friend to California but then I had to come back. I was expecting to find a job out there to make enough money to return, but I didn't have any other way to get back in a hurry."

"How long you been out on the road, son?" He'd forgotten Pauli had said she was a girl.

"Ten days exactly, sir. I'm hoping to be in New York City tonight."

"What's your name, boy?"

"Pauline. I'm a girl, sir."

"Well, I think I might believe your story, son, but I don't believe you is a girl. I'm gonna have a woman officer come and verify that."

He walked Pauli over to the office and made her wait until a female officer came and verified her gender. The officer bought her a bowl of hot soup and some bread from the diner. When she had finished eating, he came back and asked her, "So now what are you going to do, young lady?"

"I'm gonna have to get back on one of these trains, Officer."

"Well, I'll put you back on that reefer car that's goin' to Jersey City, but you be sure and stay put till you get to the station yard."

After the train pulled into the station, Pauli took the subway to her friend Toni's apartment. When Toni answered the door, she couldn't believe her eyes. "Oh my, the Lord has delivered you. You've finally come home." She looked her friend up and down. "Girl, you are as black as a chimney sweep and you smell like a swamp skunk. Lord have mercy!" She shook her head in disbelief. "Let me get you into a hot bath this minute."

Pauli smiled, almost too weak to laugh. "I think it will take more than one bath to get me clean, Toni. It's a good thing Aunt Pauline won't be seeing me like this."

Chapter 11

Women's Camp

After Pauli returned from her cross-country adventure, she made sure her aunt had returned to good health before beginning her junior year at Hunter College. Waitressing was still her primary means of supporting herself. In the summer of 1931, she worked in an oceanfront hotel in Asbury Park, New Jersey, sleeping on a cot in the laundry room to save her hard-earned cash.

In the fall she and a friend rented a furnished room near the West 137th Street branch of the YWCA. Her friend was an illustrator who received occasional assignments doing posters for upcoming Y events. Pauli worked part time at the journalism office of Hunter College. Every day, she passed the domestic workers who were forced to stand out on a street corner in the Bronx selling their labor as day workers to White women for as little as ten cents an hour. Pauli shuddered to learn its nickname: "The Bronx Slave Market."

Pauli graduated from Hunter in 1933, one of only four Black women out of 247 students in her class. She became a sales representative for *Opportunity*, the magazine of the National Urban League, an African American self-help organization. The editor at the time was Edwin A. Carter, who actively supported the young Black artists and writers whose works he published. Pauli's job was to attend social work conferences around the Midwest and South, promoting the magazine. She bought a secondhand Chevy roadster for her travels because she refused to suffer the humiliations of the segregated transportation laws in the South.

It was on one of her trips to visit her aunts that she vowed never to travel by bus below the Mason-Dixon line again. The bus had stopped at a rest area to let people use the restroom facilities. The line for the Colored restroom was too long for her to make it back to the bus in time, but no one was waiting to enter the restroom for White women. Pauli tried to be invisible as she turned the door handle to step inside. Immediately she heard a sharp rebuke from the bus driver, who was standing nearby smoking a cigarette.

"Hey there, girl, what you doin' goin' into the White ladies' restroom? You need to go, you can do it over yonder, there in the fields. I'll hold the bus for ya."

Pauli, who had probably been forced to resort to that solution many a time during her cross-country travels, this time declined on principle, preferring to endure the next two hours rather than suffer that indignity. Since overnight sleeping accommodations were all but nonexistent unless you had relatives in the area, Pauli often parked her car near the gas station where she'd filled up her tank and napped for a few hours before setting off again.

She'd held this job for a year when she became ill with pleurisy, an inflammation of the lungs. Her doctor, Mae E. Chinn, had helped her in college when she became malnourished. She warned Pauli that she was in danger of contracting tuberculosis, and recommended she go to a camp for unemployed women in Upstate New York, so Pauli decided to quit her job in order to qualify.

Camp Tera in Bear Mountain was the first of twenty-eight camps for women established during the Depression under the Temporary Emergency Relief Administration. Camps for men were already operating through the Civilian Conservation Corps, but there were none for women. Government officials assumed that most women weren't in the workforce, and those who did work outside the home could turn to their families for support if they lost a job. Some thought that putting a bunch of idle women together would encourage lesbian relations and radical political ideas. But Eleanor Roosevelt saw there was a pressing need for women's camps, and through her persistence Camp Tera was established as a test case.

Camp Tera was similar to the men's CCC, but it wasn't thought that women needed vocational training, so the camp was primarily recreational and rest oriented. Pauli considered it one step removed from being on charity, but she appreciated the numerous planned activities including arts and crafts, dramatics, hiking, rowing, and ice skating. Her appetite and health began to return as she participated in the hiking and athletic games.

Her roommate, nicknamed Pee Wee, was a pretty Black woman from Trinidad who was curious about everything. She was writing at her desk as she watched Pauli unpack a box of books and lay them on the small shelf by her bed. She marveled at the thick volume titled *Das Kapital*.

"Is that in German?" she asked, looking up from her writing.

"No, this is an English translation," Pauli answered. "But the original was in German. It was written by Karl Marx, the father of socialism and communism."

"Are you a Communist?"

"No, I'm not very well versed in political matters. I've always been more interested in literature." Pauli leafed through the heavy tome. "This book was assigned in a political science course I took in college, but I confess I didn't have time to read it. I decided to try to get through it while I'm up here with some free time on my hands." Pauli looked over at Pee Wee, who'd gone back to her writing. "How about you? What are you writing?"

"Me? Oh, I'm writing a letter to Mrs. Roosevelt to inform her that I think we need more opportunity to take training courses to develop our skills while we're recuperating at a camp like this. At the men's camps they learn vocational skills. But we just do silly arts and crafts activities like it's some kind of summer camp. We should be given the opportunity to better ourselves. For myself, I want more than anything to have a career as a recreational counselor or physical education teacher."

"Do you often write to First Ladies?"

"Not only to her—I write to anyone I think should be informed of how to make things better for folks like us. I get letters back too, sometimes." She brightened. "Say, did you hear that Mrs. Roosevelt is coming to Camp Tera next week on an inspection tour?"

"Yes, I'm looking forward to seeing her very much. She is very aware of the Negro's struggle and has done much for our cause."

"I'm sure that camp director, ol' Miss Vinegar Mills, will be running around telling everyone to spruce up the place to show it off, and trying to act so important when she comes."

"Just call me Peter Pan."

Pauli didn't much like Miss Mills either. She'd been an ambulance driver in WWI, and she strutted around the camp managing it like a military compound. Even though they were all grown women, it was Miss Mills's policy not to let the "patients" interact socially with the counselors.

Pauli had struck up a friendship with a pretty blonde woman named Peg Holmes, who led invigorating hikes up into the mountains. She was the daughter of a wealthy banker, but was a staunch supporter of civil rights and knew all about the history of the abolitionists who worked tirelessly to end slavery before the Civil War.

Sometimes the two women took an evening stroll, stopping at a secluded rock overlooking the lake. Sitting side by side, looking out over the water, Pauli shared some of the poems she was working on. Many of her poems depicted lives of unending struggle against injustice, but in one she wrote in New York in 1933, she sounded hopeful:

> Let us laugh—not in deceit,
> Not in childish pleasure—but out of gladness,—
> Joy in our youth, pride in our strength. [...]
> Let us never cease to laugh, to live, to love and to grow.

"Oh, Pauli, how can you be so optimistic? From hearing what you've written about the suffering of your people, I would be bitter if I had to face those injustices." Peg placed her arm around Pauli's shoulders and gave her a squeeze in solidarity.

Pauli wasn't used to being affectionately touched, not since Grandmother Cornelia took her in her lap when she was a child. Her "General Sourpuss" aunt had never been one to indulge in comforting hugs. Pauli looked up, surprised, meeting Peg's searching gaze in embarrassment before looking away. She closed her notebook and slid down off the rock, dusting off her khaki hiking shorts.

"Maybe I wrote that because I've been feeling a new sense of joy out here at Camp Tera."

The two women walked slowly back to camp with a new feeling of kinship. But knowing that "Miss Vinegar" frowned on counselors fraternizing with participants, they parted ways before they could be observed.

On the Sunday Mrs. Roosevelt was due to arrive, Pee Wee was

watching for her entourage to come up the driveway, but she saw only an old coupe enter the front gate. As the car came closer, Pee Wee called out, "Look, it's the First Lady herself at the wheel!"

Pauli had never been so close to such an important person before, especially not someone she so respected. She wanted to make a good impression. She rushed back to her room and changed into a freshly ironed blouse. She washed her face and combed her short light-brown locks. She felt her stomach churn with butterflies as she walked to the common room where some of the girls were waiting for Mrs. Roosevelt to come through. Pauli brought a book so as not to appear too expectant, and sat on a bench in front of a reading table.

As they approached the common room, Pauli and Pee Wee could hear Miss Mills's imperious voice chattering away at a high decibel. When the First Lady entered, Pauli felt a shiver crawl up her spine. She knew she was in the presence of a truly great woman, a woman who had genuine compassion and concern for regular folks. This would not be the last time Pauli would encounter Mrs. Roosevelt. On this occasion, she didn't want to appear to be staring so she lowered her eyes respectfully as the great lady passed by.

Immediately after the tour and visit concluded, Miss Mills called Pauli into her office.

"Miss Murray," the woman glared from behind her desk, "do you know why I have called you into my office?"

"No, I don't, Miss Mills."

"I called you into my office to reprimand you for your insolent behavior when the First Lady came through the common room. Do you know what I am referring to?"

"No, ma'am, I don't." Pauli's calm voice masked her inner turmoil and outrage.

"Likely not, so I will tell you," Miss Mills responded imperiously. "You failed to stand at attention when Mrs. Roosevelt entered the room."

"But, Miss Mills," Pauli protested, "we were not being introduced.

I was making myself as inconspicuous as I could. I have nothing but respect for Mrs. Roosevelt. I went to my room beforehand to change into fresh clothes so I could show her my best."

"Well, no amount of grooming can make up for bad behavior. Your actions will be monitored closely from now on."

A few weeks later, Pauli was called again into Miss Mills's office.

"I don't suppose you have any idea why I have called you into my office this time, Miss Murray?"

"I can't say I do, Miss Mills."

"Don't be smart with me. I tell you, I won't have any Communists in my camp."

"Communists? I don't understand," Pauli stammered in disbelief.

"One of the students found this book in your room and brought it to me." Miss Mills held out the heavy volume of *Das Kapital*.

"That book was assigned to me in college, Miss Mills. I never got the chance to read it. If I was a Communist, Miss Mills, I'm sure I would defend my right to be one, but I know nothing about communism."

"That is just the kind of attitude we don't need here at Camp Tera. I am recommending your dismissal from the camp and there will be no appeals. You will leave on the first bus out of here in the morning."

There was nothing Pauli could do but go back to her room and pack her bags. Pee Wee walked her to the bus in the morning and waved goodbye, vowing to write a letter to someone about her unfair dismissal.

Pauli went back to the city and began teaching literacy and other classes through the WPA, the Works Projects Administration started by President Roosevelt to give jobs to the unemployed during the Depression. For four years she taught classes at the Brotherhood of Sleeping Car Porters, St. James Presbyterian Church, the West 187th Street Y, and the Henry Street Settlement House. She had attended

the Brooklyn Labor College in
preparation for her teaching
assignments, but knew she
would need additional training
to find real employment when
the WPA program ended in
1938.

Pauli's friendship with Peg
Holmes continued after Peg left
Camp Tera a month after Pauli
had been ousted. She stayed
with Pauli in a small art studio
an artist friend of Pauli's allowed
her to sleep in overnight, but
the two women had to be out
of the studio during the day. To
escape the cramped spaces and
get to know each other better,
they embarked on a five-week
hitchhiking tour to Nebraska.

Girlfriend Peg standing by the rail at
Bailey's Beach, 1937.

Pauli continued to wear her Scout uniform and Peg usually wore
a skirt, so they were often regarded as a couple, but their racial status
must have caused curiosity. In a different time, they might have
gotten more scrutiny, but during the Depression people were used
to encountering the odd stranger in need of help. Defying gender
roles, the two women chopped wood and mowed lawns, and did
other menial work in exchange for a hot meal and an overnight bunk.
Riding in cars and farmers' wagons, they sought a Salvation Army or
police station in small towns to spend the night, but sometimes they
camped in the woods, availing themselves of a fresh stream to bathe
in.

Pauli hoped their close contact would create a bond that would
go beyond mere friendship. However close they were in those

years, writing and visiting each other even when they lived in different cities, Peg would eventually marry and move to California. The way Pauli saw it, she wasn't "man enough" for Peg. This realization was gravely disappointing to Pauli. The heartache and bewilderment Pauli experienced when her crushes on women were not reciprocated in the way she hoped often sent her into an emotional tailspin that sometimes ended in hospitalization for a nervous breakdown.

Pauli and Peg showing off.

By now, Aunt Pauline was sixty-eight years old and still teaching school, hoping to last until a retirement program was put in place for teachers in North Carolina so she could receive pension benefits. To appease Southern Democrats, the Social Security Act of 1935 had deliberately excluded occupations that Black people depended on, like sharecroppers, domestic workers, and teachers.

Aunt Pauline tried to convince Pauli to return to Durham. "Life is not so hard here as it is in New York," she said.

"Aunt Pauline, I would so much like to be nearer to you, to be there when you need me. But after living up North, I just don't think I can live again under the Jim Crow system. Life here 'ain't no crystal stair,' as Langston Hughes says in his poem, *A Dream Deferred*. But at least there is a measure of dignity to daily life."

However, for her aunt's sake, she took the bold step of applying to the University of North Carolina (UNC) to study sociology. She might have applied to the North Carolina College for Negroes in Durham, but they didn't have a graduate program in sociology. She hoped UNC, with its forward-thinking White president, Dr. Frank P. Graham, would open its doors to her.

Before she received a response, the Supreme Court ruled on a case brought by the National Association for the Advancement of Colored People (NAACP) on behalf of a young African American man named Lloyd Gaines, who had applied to the University of Missouri Law School and been rejected. Since there was no law school for African Americans in Missouri, the state university offered to pay for Gaines to attend an integrated law school out of state. Gaines refused, and the NAACP took his case all the way to the highest court, which ruled that since there was no segregated law school he could attend in the state, the University of Missouri was obligated to admit him.

Pauli immediately wrote Gaines a letter congratulating him and encouraging him to accept his admission, even though he would have to suffer ill treatment from the White students and staff— new laws do not always guarantee that people's minds and actions will be changed. When the day came for Lloyd Gaines to enroll, he disappeared. Perhaps he slunk into obscurity because he did not want to endure the lonely hardship of being where he was not wanted, perhaps he had received threats to his life, or maybe he was actually murdered. That mystery has never been solved.

Pauli received a letter from the University of North Carolina stating that she could not be admitted, but that "it is expected that positive action will be taken in the next session of the General Assembly to make provisions for graduate instruction for Negroes." That wasn't going to help her right now. Although Pauli met with future Supreme Court Justice Thurgood Marshall, the NAACP did not take up Pauli's case because she was not a resident of North Carolina at the time of her application, a precedent that the Gaines case had established.

Chapter 12

Bus Ride and Jail

After being denied entry to the University of North Carolina, Pauli wrote home to say that she and her girlfriend were planning to spend the Easter holiday in Durham. Pauli had met Adeline McBean when they were both teaching at the Worker's Education Project at the WPA. They decided to live together to share the rent on a two-room flat in Harlem. Adeline McBean had grown up in Harlem, the daughter of West Indian immigrants. Pauli admired Adeline's independence and spunk, but she wasn't sure how she would handle the restrictions of the segregated South.

"I've never traveled in the South," said Adeline. "But I've always been curious to know if it's as bad as people say it is."

"I don't know, Mac," Pauli answered with her nickname for Adeline. "You have such a proud, assertive manner. I'm not so sure you would be able to stomach the way of life down South. You're always saying Negroes are too timid and don't stand up for their rights."

"Well, that's certainly true, Petey," Adeline answered with her own nickname for Pauli. "My philosophy is, you never know what you are going to get if you don't push the status quo a little bit and ask for it."

"You might get into trouble is what you'll get," Pauli warned. "They don't like 'uppity' folks down there."

But Adeline insisted, and so they went. They planned to stop in Washington, DC, to visit Pauli's sister Mildred and borrow her car for the journey south. Mildred had become a nurse, like their mother Agnes, and was now head nurse at the Freedman's Hospital. Mildred cooked them a delicious meal and packed lots of provisions for their journey. She knew they would not be able to stop at any of the Whites Only restaurants on the way. But when they sat down to eat, Mildred said, "I'm sorry, Pauline, I think you'll have to ride the hated bus to Durham after all. I had to take the car to the mechanic to get a new radiator. It wouldn't have been safe for you to drive it. It won't be out of the shop for a few days."

"I wish we had time to wait for the repair. I guess we'll have to endure the indignities of the Virginia transportation system." Pauli took a final swig from her glass of milk and turned to her friend, "Well, Mac, you're in for an eye-opener."

There were no problems on the bus ride to Richmond, Virginia. There were lots of seats open in the back of the bus, so they could have their pick. Adeline settled in, adjusting the reclining chair. "This is great," she said. "These tall seats will help my back, which has been acting up lately. I'm going to doze off right now. I don't know what you're so worried about, Petey."

"Well, we haven't made our transfer yet, Mac," Pauli fretted.

Sure enough, in Richmond the 5:30 p.m. connection was already full. Another bus was being brought to the station to accommodate the rest of the passengers, taking them to a point further south where they could reboard the Durham bus after it let off some of its riders. They waited forty-five minutes for the additional bus to arrive—an old, broken-down thing with fewer seats than the first bus. The only seats available in the back were directly over the wheels, though there were plenty of open seats up front where the White passengers were sitting.

The driver made good speed to try to catch up with the Durham bus ahead. Each time the bus took a curve, Adeline and Pauli were thrown to the side. Adeline started having trouble with her back and the careening ride increased her discomfort. She saw that there were two empty seats just behind the driver.

"Look, Petey, see those two empty seats up there. Let's just go sit there."

"Have you lost your mind, Mac?" Pauli hissed sharply. "Only White people can sit in the front seats."

"Well, I have to do something," said Adeline. "I'm going to have to get off this bus; the pain is hurting me so bad with my legs scrunched up like this. Can't you ask the bus driver if we can change seats?"

Pauli let out a repressed sigh. "I'll see what I can do." She pursed her lips grimly and felt a well of dread rise in her stomach. She made her way to the driver, aware of the stares that followed her down the narrow aisle between the frayed green leather seats.

"Mister Driver, my friend is ill. The cramped seats above the wheels are causing her a great deal of pain. I was wondering if two of the White passengers could take these seats up here next to you so we could move up to the next row."

The driver, a burly fellow with a round red face, stuck his elbow out and pushed her back. He growled, "Girl, you get out of my face now and go sit back down if you know what's good for you."

"Excuse me, sir, but my friend is in pain. She has a chronic back problem."

"Not my concern, gal. What is she doing riding a bus if she's sick? Nobody is changing seats until we get to Petersburg."

Pauli slunk back to her seat, upset with herself for even attempting to reason with the man, even though she did it for the sake of her friend. They rode in fuming silence until Petersburg, where most of the White passengers disembarked. Outside they could see about twenty Black passengers preparing to board. They were all carrying picnic baskets as though ready for an outing.

"We better choose our seats now, Petey," Adeline laughed, "before those folks on their way to a church social take up all the seats in the back."

They tried the next row, but the seat by the window had fallen down and they couldn't readjust it. They went up to the next row, still two rows behind the first seat reserved for Whites. After he'd finished with the ticket-taking, the driver turned his attention to figuring out how the racial quota system would be enacted in the small world of his touring bus.

"Hey, you two back there," he called out. "You're gonna hafta move back."

"Sir, the seat behind us is broken. We can't sit on it," Adeline responded in a loud, clear voice.

"Well, you're gonna hafta find a way. You're not stayin' in those two seats. I got too many passengers comin' on board." The driver turned away for a minute. He made no effort to see whether he could fix the seat. When he turned around, he saw that the two women had stayed in the same seats.

"You back there. Did you hear what I told you? You need to move, or I'll have you both arrested for violatin' the law."

Then Adeline answered in her finest Northern stage voice, laced with a hint of British West Indies haughtiness, "Mr. Driver, I paid my money for this journey, like every other passenger on this rattletrap bus, and I am aware of my rights. My illness prevents me from riding in the seat over the wheel, nor can I ride on the seat behind us as it is hanging precariously from its hinges. I will offer to leave this purveyance if you will kindly refund the money I paid and return my baggage, which is currently on the bus ahead of us."

The driver pretended not to hear. The other passengers, who had been totally silent during Adeline's speech, resumed their hushed murmurings of disbelief at her audacity. The driver marched out of the bus with heavy steps. He stayed away for forty-five minutes while the crowd of picnickers shifted their feet on the platform outside and a small crowd of White men, who smelled trouble, loitered nearby.

"Mac, this is not a good situation," said Pauli. "We need to get word to my aunt if anything happens to us."

"What are you talking about?"

"I said, If anything happens to us," Pauli repeated firmly without trying to explain her alarm. She tore a piece of paper out of her notebook and carefully wrote Pauline Dame's name and address. Then she turned to the Black passengers in seats behind her.

"Excuse me, are any of you getting off in Durham?"

"I'll be goin' there, ma'am," one gentleman offered.

"May I ask if you would please see—if for some reason we don't make it to Durham—would you please see that my Aunt Pauline Dame is informed? Please ask her to wire Walter White of the NAACP in New York City immediately."

Pauli looked out the window and saw that the waiting Black passengers had been put on another bus that had just arrived. So there would be no issue of crowding, but Pauli was worried about those White men still hanging around outside.

Finally, the driver returned with two policemen. One of them was so fat his stomach brushed the seats as he lumbered down the aisle. The other was thin and dressed impeccably in polished black boots.

Pauli remained silent, but it seemed as though Adeline had been waiting for this moment. She stared straight at the officer, ready for whatever he gave her.

"I'm Officer Andrews," the thin officer stated. "What seems to be the trouble here?"

"Do you really have to ask me that, Officer?" Adeline began. "The trouble here is only what has been caused by the intransigence of this driver and the Virginia transportation system. Don't think you can scare me, coming in here with your brass buttons and shiny boots. I know my rights. I told the driver several times that I was ill, and I was not going to ride over the wheel or sit in any broken seats that he has not even bothered to repair." Barely pausing for breath, she continued, "If I was a White woman and told the driver I was ill, I would have been given every consideration. What I want to know is why I was not given the same consideration as a representative of the Negro race. That is what this trouble is all about!"

The officers whispered to each other, then went outside again, the fat one laboring to turn around so he wouldn't have to back out of the bus.

After a while, Officer Andrews climbed back on the bus. He approached the two women and said, "I have warrants for your arrest. Give me your names and addresses."

"May I see the warrants, please, Officer?" Pauli quickly asked.

Officer Andrews ignored her request. He walked back to the front of the bus to confer with the driver. When he returned, he leaned familiarly toward the two women, placing his arm on the top of the seat in front of them. "Look here, you two, I don't want any more trouble than we've already got, but it is my duty to carry out Virginia law. The law requires that Coloreds fill the bus starting from the rear. I didn't make the law, but that's the rule and there's nothing you can do about it. We are willing to meet you halfway if you will just move back one seat."

"But, Officer Andrews, that seat is broken," Adeline insisted.

Officer Andrews glanced back and saw that the woman was telling the truth. He called to the driver, "Mr. Morris, could you step back here please?"

Morris begrudgingly worked on the seat for a while and eventually got it back in place. The two women prepared to move back, Adeline punctuating their movement with, "If the seat had been attended to earlier, we might all be in Durham right now."

"Officer, I think we are owed an apology by Mr. Morris for the discourteous manner in which the situation was handled," said Pauli.

"Look, I just want everyone to have a square deal," said the officer testily as he walked back to the front of the bus. As he passed the driver, he stopped to hand him the arrest warrants. He spoke in a voice they could hear all the way in the back, "You hang on to these warrants here, Mr. Morris. In case there's any more trouble, you can make a citizen's arrest."

Morris settled his large behind into the driver's seat and started the ignition. The bus was now almost two hours behind schedule. A few more White passengers got on the bus and one of them took the seats Pauli and Adeline had been in, effectively changing the boundary of the "back of the bus."

The driver suddenly opened the door again as if he'd forgotten something and, leaving the engine idling, stepped down out of the bus and went back into the bus station. He came back with a stack of white cards and, moving down the aisle, distributed them among the White passengers, asking them to fill in their names and addresses and return the cards to him. When he reached the last White passengers he turned around and went forward, ignoring all the Black passengers in the rear of the bus.

Pauli leaned over and read the card held by the man in the seat in front of her. It was a form used in case of an accident, providing a space for a brief description of what happened and a space for a signature indicating willingness to testify in the event of a lawsuit. Pauli whispered through clenched teeth, "Mac, I have been tolerating the behavior of this ignorant bus driver and those two witless policemen, but I cannot stand for the total dismissal of the citizenship of the Negroes on this bus. They should be able to testify too. I have to say something."

"Pauli, dear, we are just getting on our way now. Do you have to?" Adeline queried helplessly, but then answered her own question. "Yes, I know," she sighed. "Do what you think is best."

Pauli called out, "Driver Morris, I'd like to know why you did not hand out a card to us here in the rear of the bus."

Morris did not even answer. He fairly flew off the bus and returned with the two police officers in tow. Meanwhile, Pauli had stuffed a small flashlight, notepaper, and pencils in the pockets of her raincoat. The police officers almost ran down the aisle.

"We have warned you about creating a disturbance. We're placing you under arrest. The charge is disorderly conduct and creating a public disturbance. You and your friend will have to come with us."

Pauli stood up and grabbed her bulky typewriter, her books tied up with a leather strap, and her briefcase from the overhead rack and handed Adeline her large, round hatbox. As she made her way clumsily to the front, Adeline suddenly fainted behind her, falling onto the lap of the man sitting across from them.

"Sergeant Mayhew, I'll be needing your assistance, here," Officer Andrews called to his partner.

The fat officer tried to force his way past Pauli, who was pushing forward with all of her gear. He had to wait until she passed. They half-carried, half-dragged Adeline to the door. She stood limply until a stretcher arrived and they waited for the public wagon to take them to jail.

As Pauli passed the driver sitting in his seat, she paused for a moment, remembering that it was Easter Eve. She said, "You haven't learned a thing in two thousand years."

A neatly dressed Black man quietly approached Pauli as she came off the bus. "Tell me your name, sister, so we can keep track of you."

"Pauli Murray."

"Is there anyone you want me to notify?"

"Please, if you could wire my sister Mildred Murray in Washington, DC. Her address is in the phone book. Please notify my sister."

First they were taken to Petersburg City Hospital, where Adeline was able to recover from her fainting spell. Then they made their way to the Petersburg city prison. The authorities there were not so hospitable.

"I'd like to make my telephone call," Pauli requested.

"You won't be communicating with anyone, girl," said the desk officer, a burly man with beady blue eyes and a bald head glistening in the harsh light.

"Officer, it is the right of every person under arrest to make one phone call to a lawyer," Pauli insisted.

"Don't you come in here trying to boss me," the officer said. "We're the boss now, an' if you don't shet up, I'll set your ass in the dungeon." He leered at her from his high seat. "Time them rats down there get through with you, you'll wish you'd kep' your mouf shet."

Petersburg City Prison, Petersburg, Virginia, 1940.

Adeline gave Pauli an imploring look. All their luggage was taken away from them. They were only allowed to keep their coats, but Pauli had remembered her paper and pencil in her pocket. They were led through a hallway where men were sleeping on mats because the jail was so overcrowded. They were pushed into a narrow cell and heard the heavy door clang shut behind them. Three other women were in the cell.

Pauli later wrote to her aunts describing the surroundings:

> *A rust-encrusted sink and foul-smelling open toilet stood near the door. Close to the heavily barred windows at the other end of the cell were four double-decker iron beds pushed against the wall. Each had a grimy straw mattress, one sheet, and a grease-caked blanket. There were no towels for washing and only one bar of soap. The women were occupied in building a small smudge fire in the center of the cement floor, using scraps of paper they had saved for that purpose, to ward off the huge water bugs that crawled out of the cracks at night.*

One of the women sniffed, "You all don't seem the type to be in here. What'd they put you in for?"

"We were put off a bus for disorderly conduct when we asked to sit in a proper seat not allowed by Jim Crow."

"Whoa, that Jim Crow fella, he causes more trouble 'roun here," the woman chuckled. "Me, I was picked up for tryin' to get a little money for food with my sinful ways. Soliciting."

"I was out on the street after curfew, trying to go see my sick mama after I finished working at ol' Miz Charles's house," another soul chimed in.

"I busted a milk bottle over my man's head," a third woman proclaimed. "And he done deserve it," she added, shaking her finger at the rest of the group.

Next morning, after a breakfast of soggy pancakes and molasses, and coffee in tin cups, Pauli and Adeline surveyed their quarters. Adeline walked over to read an old typewritten sheet tacked up on the wall titled "Rules for Prisoners."

"Look at this, Petey. 'Rule No. 2. Each prisoner shall keep his person, clothing, and cell equipment clean.' I sure don't see any way to do that around here."

"We should follow Gandhi's principle of *satyagraha*, the practice of peaceful protest, wherever we see unfair conditions," said Pauli. "Let's write a letter requesting the minimum of toiletry articles to keep ourselves clean."

When the judge read out the sentence on Monday morning, the segregated courtroom was filled with two hundred fifty people, Blacks on one side of the room and Whites on the other. The conviction now included violation of a section of the segregation law. Pauli and Adeline were released on bond and their NAACP attorney asked for an appeal.

In the new trial, violation of the segregation laws was omitted; they were charged only with disturbing the peace. They had to come all the way back to Petersburg, Virginia, to hear the decision.

After a good wait, the black-robed judge walked into the court, mounted the bench, and rifled distractedly through some papers. Without ever looking at the two women sitting in the defendants' seat across the courtroom, he announced: "About those two girls, there's nothing in the brief to make me change my mind—I still fine them ten dollars each." He barely looked their way, scanning the courtroom for their lawyer. "Will you be paying the fine or staying in jail?"

Pauli stood up, this time without their lawyer, who hadn't been able to make the trip. "Respectfully, Your Honor, we don't have the money to pay the fine."

"Then it's back to jail for your sentence. Officer, handcuff them and take them away."

The deputy put them in a cell by themselves this time. A guard brought in clean mattresses and a crew, armed with mops and disinfectant, scrubbed the floor and cleaned the toilet. They even brought spray guns and an acetylene torch to burn out the bedbugs hiding in the cracks of the iron beds. After a few days, the Workers Defense League wired the money for their release.

As they stood on the steps of the jail, Adeline sighed. "I feel like the man in the Western films who says, 'I will never show my face in these parts again.' I think I've seen enough of the Jim Crow South."

Chapter 13

The Odell Case

The Workers Defense League was so impressed with Pauli's determination and commitment at the St. Petersburg trial, they asked her to come and work for them in New York. At their weekly planning meeting, one of the members who had arranged bail for Pauli introduced her to the group. "Pauli Murray will bring a new dedication and spirit to our organization. We are extremely happy to have her with us."

"I am only too glad to offer my services to the League after their help during my trial," Pauli answered before they got down to business.

"Our first agenda is a new case, that of Odell Waller," the director said. "Odell Waller has been convicted of killing his White landlord, Owen Davis, in a dispute over their jointly owned wheat crop. It seems Davis evicted Waller's wife and his mother Annie while Waller was away working another job. They were evicted from the little shack they lived in down on Davis's place. When the wheat was harvested, Davis took Waller's share and loaded it in his own barn. When Waller came home, he went to get his wheat. They got into an argument and Davis pulled out a gun. Whereupon Waller pulled out *his* gun and shot four bullets into him. Davis subsequently died and Waller was convicted of wrongful murder, but we believe he shot Davis in self-defense. We need three hundred fifty dollars before three weeks are out to file an appeal." The director looked straight at Pauli. "Since you're from the South, Miss Murray, we thought you might be the one to start gaining support in the Richmond area."

"But I have no car, sir, and I will not ride that Jim Crow bus again anytime soon."

"I have a car you can use if you don't mind a nine-year-old convertible coupe," one of the group members offered.

"I'm not sure I would want to drive alone," Pauli worried.

"I'll go with you," said a White woman named Gene. "I worked with sharecroppers in Oklahoma for the Federal Emergency Relief Administration. They get a rough deal. And besides, I've driven that ramshackle car and I know its eccentricities."

So the unlikely pair drove down to Richmond. As soon as they crossed the city line, in a foretelling of their dismal luck on the trip, they were stopped by a policeman for driving without a taillight. Fortunately, he didn't ticket them but pointed them in the direction of a repair shop. By the time they arrived at the office of Waller's defense attorney, the doors were closed, and they couldn't find his home address in the telephone directory.

"What will we do? We can't afford a hotel room," said Gene.

"You mean we can't afford two hotel rooms in two different hotels, one for you and one for me." Pauli corrected her before adding, "Wait, I have a cousin, Sadie, who might be able to take us in. She lives out on West Clay Street." Pauli seemed to have a relative in every city. They had already spent the night with her sister Grace in Baltimore.

Sadie opened the door and immediately gave Pauli a big hug, but she eyed Gene with some suspicion, slowly offering her hand in greeting. "Hello, ma'am." She turned to Pauli, "So, what brings you all here?"

"Sadie, this is my friend Gene. She's helping me in our fundraising drive for Odell Waller, the sharecropper who's been sentenced to death. We need a place to stay for the night."

"Oh, yes, what a sad story that is. Of course you can stay here."
Sadie cooked a delicious meal and gave the women her own bedroom
to sleep in. After Gene went in the room, Sadie took Pauli aside and
whispered, "Pauli, I hope you don't mind my asking, but is your friend
White or Colored?"

"She's White, Sadie."

"It's all the same to me, of course, but aren't you taking a chance
driving through the South with a White woman?"

"Please don't worry about it. We're so grateful for your help. We'll
be moving on in the morning."

After a big breakfast that would end up having to last them
the whole day, Pauli went over their plan. "You'll cover the White
neighborhoods, Gene, and I'll canvas my brothers and sisters."

"I don't know, Pauli, this whole place gives me the creeps. I don't
think I want to visit these people alone."

They hadn't known how hilly and spread out the city of Richmond
was. If they separated, only one of them would be able to use the car.
Finally, Gene said, "All right. I'll take the bus out to the labor folks
while you drive to the college and the church group where you made
arrangements to speak."

Pauli stopped her car near a passing student at Virginia Union
University, established in 1865 for the education of freed people.
"Can you show me the way to the chapel, please?"

Pauli heard the bell ring for chapel and watched the students
changing classes, crossing the green in their idyllic surroundings,
and thought with envy how much she'd rather be in school right
now. Professor Moore, with whom she'd made the arrangements,
came out of the chapel and looked startled when he saw the young
woman standing there. "Oh, you are Miss Murray? I'm—" he
hesitated "—I'm glad to meet you, Miss Murray. Will you wait a
minute in my office? No, on second thought, wait here outside the

door to the chapel. I have to see to something. I'll be right back." And he hurried off.

It started to rain as Pauli stood outside the chapel, mindful of the stares from students as they filed inside. Finally the last of the students was inside and someone came out to close the door. Only then did Professor Moore come scurrying down the path.

"I'm very sorry, Miss Murray. I've made a terrible blunder. I'm not really in charge of chapel services and I had no authority to invite you to speak. The program for Monday is already filled and there won't be time for you."

"I don't understand, sir," Pauli protested. "We spoke on the telephone and you said it was all arranged."

"That's true," the professor said, looking despondent. "I asked the committee if you could come to speak Wednesday and well, the fact is, they said no. This is a conservative school. They were not sure about your organization, the Worker's Defense League. They thought it might be associated with Communists."

Pauli stood speechless. "But I drove all the way on your say-so."

"Miss Murray, I do apologize. To tell you the truth, Miss Murray—how shall I put this?—over the telephone, I thought you were White. I was ashamed to tell you then that a Negro university wouldn't let a White woman who was speaking for the Negro cause come to speak. I hoped to confront them with the fact of you being White. I thought they would relent and let you speak when they saw you. That's why I urged you to come. But then, when I saw you were Colored, I knew the situation was hopeless."

Pauli stiffened. "Thank you, Professor Moore, for your honesty. I see that you did your best."

The unhappy man wrung his hands and finally suggested, "Would you like to come in out of the rain and join us for chapel?"

"Perhaps another time," Pauli answered icily.

Dispirited, she got into her leaky car and drove on to the Baptist Minister's Convention full of misgiving. By the time she got there she was exhausted and hungry. She felt feverish and her head was throbbing. She slipped into a seat in the back of the room and watched as the various groups came forward to press for their causes. Reverend Hill, who was presiding over the meeting and who had asked her to speak, acknowledged her presence with a nod. Finally, Dr. Leon A. Ransom of the NAACP rose to speak.

He was visiting with Thurgood Marshall, who, like Dr. Ransom, was a professor from Howard University Law School in Washington, DC. They were there with the NAACP to drum up support for four young Black men charged with rape. Their only crime was to have given a lift to a White woman who had been dumped off on the side of the road by a group of White men. Everyone knew they would most likely receive the death penalty if convicted of raping a White woman.

After Dr. Ransom's speech, the ministers came forward with their congregation's pledge to the NAACP Defense Fund, each one elaborating on the toll their contribution was taking from their church's funds. By the end of the service, they counted up a paltry ninety-five dollars. Pauli was so disheartened, she rose from her seat intending to slip away through the side door.

Reverend Hill caught sight of her and called out, "Miss Murray, where are you going?" She hesitated at the door as he walked over to her, put his arm around her shoulders, and led her to the front of the room, proclaiming loudly to the group of ministers, who were all men, "Brothers, hear me out. This young lady has a problem and I want you to hear what she has to say."

He pushed her forward without any further introduction and she stood there totally unprepared, looking at the expectant faces. She was about to faint from hunger. She tried to open her mouth to speak, but only felt the tears welling up in her eyes. She stood in silence until she could muster up the strength to say, "Gentlemen, I apologize. I have traveled a long distance. Accommodations have been difficult. I am hungry. I haven't the strength to give you any message. Reverend

Hill, perhaps you could read this statement we have prepared?"

The Reverend read in a firm, strong voice: "This is about Odell Waller, a poor sharecropper . . ."

Then Pauli stepped to the podium. "Gentlemen, I have come a long way and traveled through much adversity to help raise funds for Odell's appeal. Each person we've met has sent us to another, each one too timid to be associated with this cause. The White people refer us to the Negroes and the Negroes send us back to the White people. Why, I just came from Virginia Union College where they refused to let me speak because they didn't think a Negro could convince them to help the cause. And I drove all night to keep that engagement. I've spent almost a week without finding any member of our community who will take responsibility for helping this unknown, friendless sharecropper. If men of God, like the brothers sitting here, cannot take Waller's plight into their hearts, where are we to turn for help?"

There was a profound silence in the room when she finished. Then a small white-haired man, who was sitting by himself near the wall, rose slowly to his feet and spoke in a voice that was barely audible. "I know the young man, Odell. I am his spiritual advisor in the death house. He's a fine young feller who needs a chance. He is a hard worker, works two jobs trying to make ends meet for his mother and wife. He was working another job when old man Davis run his mother off the property."

"All right, brethren," said Reverend Hill, "you've heard the problem. What are you going to do about it? I know what I'm going to do. Lay this here dollar right down."

Without a word, one after another, the ministers came forward, each putting down a dollar. It was their own money being given now, coming out of their own pockets. One man gave seventy-five cents and another added a quarter. All told, it came to twenty-five dollars, the beginning of a nationally known cause that would eventually raise thirty thousand dollars.

As she was speaking to Dr. Ransom and some of the ministers at the end of the meeting, Thurgood Marshall waved Pauli over and said, "I was quite impressed with the appeal you made today, young lady."

Pauli laughed, "Maybe I should become a lawyer, I've had so many brushes with the law in the past two years."

"I think that would be a fine idea, Miss Murray. You have what it takes to be a good lawyer. Why not come to Howard? We'd be glad to have you."

"I might take you up on that offer if there was a scholarship to go with it."

"If you send in your application, I'll see that you get one," said Dr. Ransom.

Chapter 14

Howard Law School

Pauli sent in her application and received a scholarship to Howard University School of Law. There was only one other incoming freshman woman during Pauli's first year, and she dropped out before the end of the first term. Although two or three women enrolled after her, Pauli remained the only woman in her class for all three years. There were no women on the faculty. The only other woman who had graduated from Howard Law now worked as a registrar, an administrative position.

On the first day of class, one of Pauli's professors addressed the men in the room. "I really don't know why women come to law school, but since they're here, I guess we men will have to put up with them." All the men laughed in solidarity while Pauli whispered to her seatmate through clenched teeth, "He doesn't know it, but he just guaranteed that I would become the top student in his class."

Pauli was usually ignored when she held up her hand to answer questions. She found it difficult to engage in the freewheeling style of the male students whose voices were louder and more confident than hers. Often the professor went the rounds of all the students, searching for the correct answer to a question, and it was only after all the men had been given their chance that he would finally turn to

Pauli.

"And you, Miss Murray, do you think you can help these gentlemen out, now that the process of elimination is complete?"

Pauli, more often than not, provided the correct answer, but she was seldom given the chance to display her prowess.

One day Pauli checked the school bulletin board for announcements and saw a notice posted: "All Male Students of the First Year Class are invited to a Smoker at the Residence of Dr. Leon A. Ransom." Dr. Ransom was the professor who had originally encouraged Pauli to attend the law school. Pauli immediately went to his office.

"Dr. Ransom, I wonder if you can explain to me why your invitation specifically excludes female class members?"

"Miss Murray, Sigma Delta Tau is a legal fraternity limited to male students and members of the legal profession. The goal of the gathering, or 'smoker' as we call it, is to look over the prospects for inclusion into the fraternity. Naturally, because women cannot join the fraternity, it would have been silly to invite them."

"But, sir, membership in the fraternity is a valuable tool in fostering networks and mentoring the law student, helping him to develop contacts for his future career. What about the female candidates for the degree? Isn't that opportunity open for us too?"

Dr. Ransom smiled condescendingly and clasped his hands together on his desk. "Well, if the women need to belong to an organization, I suppose we could set up a legal sorority. How would you gals like that?"

"Sir, if I may say so, it would be ridiculous for us to set up a society that would at the present time include only two members."

"That is a sound conclusion, my dear." Dr. Ransom started shuffling through his papers. "Did you have any other concerns today, Miss Murray?"

"No, sir," said Pauli. She left his office seething with indignation.

This was only one of the incidents that made Pauli's blood rise in those days. In the summer of 1942, she received a letter from a friend in Oregon saying she was "glad for the protection of the Japanese Americans that have been evacuated." Pauli knew these citizens weren't being protected—they were rounded up because they were regarded as potential spies. This assumption so angered Pauli that she wrote a letter to the president, in care of Mrs. Roosevelt:

> *If Japanese Americans can be 'evacuated' to prevent violence being perpetrated against them, then certainly you have the power to 'evacuate' Negro citizens from 'lynching' areas in the South, and particularly in poll tax states . . . Negroes whose vote helped win your election feel you have never come out openly on the question of the Negro in this country.*

Pauli soon received a note from Mrs. Roosevelt, inviting her to tea at her apartment overlooking Washington Square in New York City.

Pauli was not totally unknown to Mrs. Roosevelt by this time. When Pauli was executive secretary of National Sharecroppers Week, she invited the First Lady to be the main speaker at the conference and bestow an award for the best student essay on democracy. Mrs. Roosevelt had invited Pauli and a few members of the committee to her apartment then, too, for tea. They were all so excited, they didn't eat any of the sweets set out on elegant silver trays. Pauli told her aunts afterward, "Whenever I spoke to Mrs. Roosevelt, she gave me her complete attention as if in that moment I was the most important person in her world."

Mrs. Roosevelt had also been involved in the Odell Waller case in its final hours, when all legal remedies of due process had not been able to secure Waller's release from death row. The NAACP lawyers had argued that Waller had not been tried by a jury of his peers because of the effect of the poll tax in Virginia. Jurors were commonly picked from the voter rolls, and in the county where Odell lived, only one-fifth of the population had paid the poll tax that would make them eligible to vote. In the end, the lawyers were not able to prove that all jurors were selected from the voter rolls, and the governor of Virginia set the date for execution. Mrs. Roosevelt petitioned her husband to pardon Waller, but the president would not rule against the governor.

Now, Mrs. Roosevelt met Pauli at the door and totally disarmed her by giving her a great big hug.

"Miss Murray, I am delighted to see you again. I am so proud of your pursuit of the law degree. The profession will never be the same with you among its members, and that can only be an improvement."

"I only hope I can do the law degree justice, Mrs. Roosevelt."

"First, I want to tell you how sorry I was to hear of Odell Waller's execution." The First Lady sighed audibly and shook her head. "That was a terrible night, wasn't it?"

"Yes, ma'am."

"But now we have some matters to discuss," Mrs. Roosevelt continued. "I invited you here because I wanted to respond in person to some of the things you said in your letter. How can you honestly compare the evacuation of Japanese, with whom we are at war, with citizens of your race who have been here as long as the White people have? Do you think they would take kindly to being separated off and treated as though they were not as rightfully here as any other people?"

"Mrs. Roosevelt, I can see that the tone of my letter was reckless. Certainly it was not intended to offer any fundamental solution to a major problem. I wrote out of desperation that there doesn't seem to be a way of bringing home to the American people our utterly untenable position of fighting in democracy's name for supremacy over the Axis powers, while thirteen million of our own citizens are victims of a racial theory as vicious as Hitler's."

Mrs. Roosevelt countered, "But you know that the president

initiated the creation of the Fair Employment Practice Committee, which indicates where the president stands on wartime jobs for Negro workers."

"If you will forgive me, Mrs. Roosevelt, although appointing that commission was certainly a step in the right direction, it was hastily put through mainly because the government was faced with a march on Washington by Negroes throughout the country, which was planned by A. Philip Randolph of the Pullman Porters Union. If anything, it seems to indicate that the president will remain aloof from the Negro question until there is such organized resentment and pressure as to make it a national embarrassment if he does not act."

"But you don't realize," the First Lady insisted, "that on the day a man is elected president, he has to take into consideration the people who are the heads of important committees in Congress, none of whom he has chosen but with whom he must work and on whom he must depend to pass vital legislation for the nation as a whole . . . and that they often," she added ruefully, "refuse to pass."

After much discussion and respectful give-and-take, Pauli left with a feeling that Mrs. Roosevelt was listening to her concerns. But two weeks later, in early September 1942, at the International Student Assembly, their relationship again became tense. Mrs. Roosevelt was presiding over the Assembly to make sure all the representatives from Allied countries remained in harmony, and Pauli was attending as a delegate from Howard.

Two members of the Soviet delegation, a man and a woman, caused quite a stir in their military uniforms. Along with the British, the Soviets had been pressing to open up a second front in Europe. The American delegation was sponsoring platforms dealing with human rights, specifically calling for an end to colonial rule in India by the British, and denouncing Soviet imperialism in the Baltic state of Lithuania. African American members of the US delegation were circulating a statement calling for the destruction of the doctrine of race supremacy.

In the receiving line at the picnic held on the White House lawn, Mrs. Roosevelt clasped Pauli's hands between her strong palms, looking forcefully into the younger woman's face, and said, "Pauli, I want to talk to you later."

Pauli tried to avoid the First Lady, keeping her at a safe distance until Mrs. Roosevelt finally cornered her on the far side of the lawn.

"Pauli, I urge you not to push for the resolutions on India and Lithuania. There is a rumor that the Russian and British student representatives might walk out and disrupt the proceedings. You must understand that the goal of the conference is to show unity between the countries allied to combat the Axis powers, Germany, Italy, and Japan."

"I understand your concern, Mrs. Roosevelt, but this assembly is also about the voices of private citizens speaking out on human rights. That will be an issue no matter what else is going on in the war. I will keep your concerns in mind, though."

As it turned out, there was no Lithuanian platform, but a resolution on India was presented. This resolution would be very similar to the resolution in the Universal Declaration of 1948 of the United Nations which would be put forth by the First Lady herself. It called for the recognition of "the principle of independence for colonials and equal rights and opportunities for national, religious, and racial minorities" and the "abolition of all discriminations based solely on race, color, creed, or national origin." The delegates pushing for a human rights platform had succeeded. Pauli returned to her studies with some satisfaction.

When Pauli moved to Washington, her girlfriend Mac came with her, enrolling in undergraduate classes of her own at Howard. Mac had a way of following in Pauli's footsteps. Pauli had been able to spend the summer in a two-room cabin in the Catskill Mountains in New

York at a summer camp for the Young People's Socialist League in exchange for giving a few lectures on the sharecropper situation. She hoped to use the time to work on her writing. She had always had a desire to write, but knew she would be unable to earn a living that way. Never shy about approaching famous people, she'd sent some of her poems and stories to the poet Stephen Vincent Benét, who was known for his epic poem about the Civil War. He encouraged Pauli to turn her own experiences and family history into fiction. She thought she would be alone with her German shepherd Petie but, true to form, Mac managed to get a job at a health facility nearby so she could spend time at the camp too.

By the end of Pauli's first year at Howard, the two women decided not to live together. Pauli was hoping to find accommodations on campus so she wouldn't have to lug her heavy law books around, but the university did not provide housing for graduate students. Fortunately, the cousin who had found Pauli a job at the 137th Street YWCA in Harlem was now dean of women at Howard, and she managed to find a tiny space for Pauli in the freshman women's dormitory. The building was named Sojourner Truth Hall after the Black abolitionist who made her famous speech at the Ohio Women's Rights Convention in 1851 called "Ain't I a Woman?" Pauli managed to fit a cot, a bookshelf, and a trunk filled with clothes and papers in the small room equipped with a sink and toilet. The room was next to a large sitting area used for social occasions where Pauli was able to study.

After a while, the young undergraduates learned of the older law student in their midst who knew a lot about civil rights, and they began holding late night strategy sessions about ways to combat segregation in Washington, DC. As they planned actual protests, including sit-ins at local restaurants during WWII, Pauli devised a questionnaire to determine students' commitment to the cause. One of the questions was "Am I a 'screwball,' or am I a pioneer?" They were also asked if the "struggle for equal rights" should be postponed until the war ended. Ninety percent of the respondents said "no," and eighty percent said they wished to participate in some kind of action.

The District of Columbia didn't have any segregation laws, but separation of the races by habit and custom continued. Transportation was integrated, but African Americans were not welcome in many public spaces including hotels, restaurants, and theaters and they couldn't buy homes in traditionally White neighborhoods. Most restaurants in Black neighborhoods were integrated, but one establishment near Howard University had a "White Trade Only" sign in the window, which was especially offensive to the students. The students chose the Little Palace Cafeteria as their first target for protest.

About twenty students participated on April 27, 1943, entering the cafeteria in groups of three, approaching the food bar with their trays. When the students pointed to the food and requested their choices, the Black servers stared at them in disbelief and made no move to serve them. So, they carried their empty trays to vacant tables without saying a word. The students opened their textbooks and notebooks and began to study as more of their group entered and went through the same drill.

Other students formed a picket line outside. One of their signs proclaimed, "WE DIE TOGETHER. WHY CAN'T WE EAT TOGETHER?" A White supporter began to informally ask the White patrons what they thought about the protest.

One woman said, "I'm from Charlotte, North Carolina. I eat here regularly and I don't care who eats here. All I want is to eat my food."

Another man said, "I want the place to stay open. After all, we are all human."

"I think it's reasonable. Negroes are fighting to win the war for democracy, just like the Whites."

"If it came to a vote, it would get my vote."

An hour later, the owner, Mr. Chaconas, closed the cafeteria as the tables filled up with nonpaying students. He told a reporter, "I'll lose money, but I'd rather close up than practice democracy this way. The time is not ripe."

On Monday morning, he tried to reopen the restaurant but found the picketers still marching with their signs out front. Potential customers walked on by when they saw the raucous activity. Two days later, Mr. Chaconas gave in and started serving all customers.

Although the mostly female students were elated by their successful sit-in, Pauli was overcome by the stress of completing her coursework at the top of her class while organizing the protest. She checked in to the infirmary for six days of rest and recuperation. For such a strong, adventurous woman, Pauli often suffered breakdowns when she worked herself too hard, didn't eat enough, and experienced emotional issues regarding her relationships with women. Two years before, when she'd realized her friendship with Peg Holmes would never lead anywhere—Peg was moving to California to get married—Pauli hitchhiked to Massachusetts to see her one last time.

On a stop in Providence, Rhode Island, a kindly policewoman found the boyishly dressed woman wandering the streets. To explain her appearance, Pauli told the woman she was a lesbian and was disoriented because she was taking hormones. The officer personally drove her back to New York City, depositing her at police headquarters, where she was promptly taken to Bellevue Hospital for psychiatric care. An FBI report on Pauli Murray later noted that she was diagnosed with schizophrenia because she believed she was a man. Fortunately, her friend Mac was able to get her released by pretending to be her cousin.

Her primary doctor, who had recommended she convalesce at Camp Tera, checked her in to a private facility for further examination.

"I know I'm overworked, Dr. Chinn," Pauli explained. "I haven't been able to eat or sleep. I've been upset over the disappearance of a friend." Pauli wrung her hands in her lap. "You see, when I fall in love with a woman, I don't have any chance to express my attraction in normal ways."

"What do you mean by normal?" Dr. Chinn asked.

"Normal is a heterosexual male in love with a heterosexual female."

"Yes, but we can have close, even physical affection for people of our own sex."

"But I don't think I am a lesbian, Dr. Chinn. It's something physical about me. The only people who accept me as I am are people who know me well, like my aunt Pauline. She accepts me pretty much as one of nature's experiments—a girl who should have been a boy."

Pauli was quiet for a moment before continuing. "Dr. Chinn, I think I might not have enough female hormones. Or maybe I have a male organ hiding inside of me. Isn't there some way I could be tested?"

Dr. Chinn, like other doctors Pauli had consulted, thought her troubles were psychological. She didn't prescribe any tests.

This time, in the Howard infirmary, Pauli felt it was the same old trouble repeating itself. She wrote her aunt about her situation:

> It began when a young sophomore sort of walked into my life without my realizing what was happening to me. This person was rather shocked when she learned how I felt about her. Some gossip had started around campus. Mother, I've done nothing of which to be ashamed, but I do admit that my 'boy-girl' personality, as you jokingly call it, sometimes gets me into trouble . . . I try to live by society's standards, but doing so causes me such inner conflict that at times it's almost unbearable . . . This conflict rises up to knock me down at every apex I reach in my career.

Pauli told a friend that her "crack-up" was serious.

"What do you mean?" her friend asked. "I thought you were only in the infirmary six days for bed rest."

"I couldn't take my exams. I was so worried I would have to leave

Howard, I applied to the University of Michigan law school!" Pauli exclaimed. "But Dean Ransom wouldn't let me go. What a sweetheart. He said I could postpone my second-year exams until September, right before classes start." Pauli shook her head. "I declare, sometimes I wonder whether I'm a 'screwball or a pioneer,' like I asked the students in my questionnaire."

True to her prediction, even before taking the exams, Pauli ranked at the top of her class. At the end of her first year, Pauli's standing in the class ensured that she was elected associate justice of the Court of Peers by the Law Students Guild. After taking her exams, she had the highest grade-ranking in the second-year class. When the grades were posted, the only other two female law students rushed up to Pauli and said, "Congratulations, honey, you're sure to be elected chief justice of the Court of Peers. You have to be!"

Pauli smiled. "Well, I'll see it before I believe it. You know how male-dominated the school is." But inwardly she felt sure the position would fall to her.

Pauli eagerly looked for signs announcing the upcoming election for chief justice. But no signs were posted around campus as they had been the year before, not even for the associate justice. Pauli asked a friend to make some inquiries.

Finally her friend Henry came to her room with a sad face.

"Pauli, you're not going to like this."

"Tell me," Pauli sighed.

"They're not going to hold elections at all this year. They've disbanded the Court of Peers." Henry stared at the floor.

"They what? I can't believe it." Pauli paced around the room, containing her anger the way she always did when faced with blatant unfairness. "They are just going to leave the position vacant because they won't give it to the most qualified student—who happens to be a woman?"

Henry looked up hopefully. "Are you going to fight the injustice, like you always do?"

"No, Henry," Pauli shrugged. "At least they didn't pick the second best. They are the ones who are losing out this year. I'll grin and bear it like I usually do around here. I'll concentrate on my studies. Remember, we have to take Professor Spottswood's Bills and Notes this term, one of the most challenging courses in the school."

"Last year old 'Spots' failed nine of the fifteen students in the class," Henry reminded her. "And this year, we have to take it with the second-year students because so many are being drafted into Uncle Sam's segregated army," Henry added. "They can't fill up two classes."

"We have to learn a mass of technical rules governing checks, promissory notes, drafts, bills of lading, and other commercial documents in various jurisdictions," said Pauli. "And we have to prepare daily cases and materials. Not to mention being responsible for Spots's detailed lectures. If we fall behind, we'll be in a boat without a paddle."

"Did you know Bill Jones will be taking the class?" Henry asked. "He's coming back as a second-year because he lost a year due to his eye problems."

Pauli was sitting next to Bill Jones in class the next day when he whispered to her, "Pauli, it's coming back. My blindness. I can't see the words on the page."

"Oh, Billy, I'm so sorry." Pauli touched his arm. "My grandfather was blind toward the end of his life. I learned to read by reading him the newspaper aloud. I'd lie on the porch floor at his feet while he rocked in his favorite rocking chair."

"I'm going to have to leave the class."

"What can I do to help?"

"Take some good notes, Pauli. I'll need them if I'm ever to catch up. I'll have to leave school for a while."

Bill did come back before the term ended, determined to pass Bills and Notes. "I'm not doing this again, Pauli. This course is worse than being blind," he said as another classmate walked by.

"We're forming a study group, Pauli. Will you join us?" the classmate said, staring straight at Pauli as he spoke. He didn't even seem to see Bill.

"I'll see," said Pauli, embarrassed for her friend. "And Billy, too?"

"Oh, gosh," the student said, finally turning toward Billy. "I really admire your guts coming back and tackling this course after your illness, but I think you might drag down the study group since you have so much to catch up on. You probably need a special tutor."

"Well, thanks for asking," Pauli said. "We have to run now."

While they were walking, Pauli couldn't help thinking about her grandfather, whose eye was injured when he fought in the Civil War. She had seen him gradually lose his sight over the years. She put her mind to thinking and came up with an idea.

"Billy, you need a tutor, right? You can't read on your own, you'll strain your eyes. What if I read aloud to you? Don't they say the best way to learn is to teach? I'm going to read aloud and we'll both memorize the lessons. But we'll have to follow a strict regimen. And we'll have to do it outside, because we'll be too noisy, otherwise."

So the two of them walked everywhere together, to and from class, to the cafeteria, to the library. They walked up Georgia Avenue, sidestepping children and their mothers, and old men on the street, oblivious to their surroundings as they cited endless Bills and Notes.

When the Bills and Notes grades were posted on the bulletin board a few days after the term ended, Pauli rushed to the hall where they were displayed. She was astounded to discover that her grade was ninety-five.

"What did I get?" Billy tugged her sleeve, close behind her.

"Oh, my stars, Billy. You got an eighty-five! You're second in the rank. And the next highest grade is a seventy!"

The Law Student Guild called a special meeting to bring back the Court of Peers in order to elect Pauli Murray as chief justice. Bill Jones ended his career as a judge in East St. Louis, Missouri.

Chapter 15

Sitting In

Pauli continued her civil rights activities, even though it was challenging during her third and final year at the law school. The Howard University campus supported a chapter of the NAACP, and the students continued to plan their strategy for the next protest.

"We managed to get the Little Palace Cafeteria to serve us, but that was in our own neighborhood. Now we have to strike out downtown," Pauli said.

"Let's go after Thompson's Cafeteria," one of the more plucky students suggested.

Another student chimed in. "Yes. They've got three restaurants, but the one at 11th and Pennsylvania would be the best. It's open twenty-four hours a day and employees who work late at the Post Office could use a place to eat. Hell, we'd be helping the restaurant get more business."

At 4 p.m. on a sunny Saturday afternoon on April 22, 1944, a few plucky Howard students sauntered into Thompson's Cafeteria in groups of twos and threes, each group coming in about ten minutes after the previous group.

Outside, one woman spat at the picketers. White soldiers yelled catcalls. Some of the people passing by supported the students, and a few female enlistees from the WACs (Women's Army Corps) and WAVES (Women's Naval Reserves) cheered them on. One of their signs read, "Are you for HITLER'S WAY (Race Supremacy) or the AMERICAN WAY (Equality)?"

Six African American soldiers, unaffiliated with the protest, walked by and decided to enter the restaurant requesting service. Their corporal's and sergeant's stripes adorned their crisp, starched uniforms. When the servers ignored them, they sat down like the Howard students at empty tables and began to read the newspaper. White soldiers were eating nearby. Within the hour, fifty-six demonstrators and the six Black soldiers were sitting at tables. The manager approached a group at one table. "Please, this is not my policy, but we are losing business here," he said.

Then the district supervisor for Thompson's entered the premises telling the students, "We will take this under advisement with our head office, but you really need to go now."

In a little while, two White military policemen came up to the Black soldiers sitting at the table with empty trays.

"Please, it would be best if you officers quietly got up and left the restaurant so as not to embarrass the United States Army during a time of war."

"We're just waiting for service, sir," they answered.

A White lieutenant returned with another MP. "I apologize for the trouble here, but as a personal favor to the US Army, we are asking that you please vacate the premises so the army won't be embarrassed in case of an incident."

Pauli overheard this conversation from a nearby table. She quickly walked up to the table. "May I interject, sir? If the Army is afraid of being embarrassed, perhaps you should request that all military personnel leave."

The lieutenant looked over at the White soldiers who were finishing up their meals. "You've got a point there, Miss." He immediately went over to the soldiers' table and informed them that they'd better be going, too. "You don't mind, do ya, fellas? We're trying not to create an incident here."

Meanwhile, the manager was making frantic calls to Thompson's main office in Chicago. "Business has dropped fifty percent. What are we going to do? These picketers could be back tomorrow."

At 8:30 p.m., a call from headquarters came telling the manager to order the waiters to serve the Black customers. Two White waitresses refused. After they were spoken to by the manager, they walked out, and the managers had to take their places as servers.

The students couldn't believe how easy it was. For the next few days, a few select students were able to get a meal at Thompson's Cafeteria, but then suddenly they were refused again. Howard's president, Mordecai Johnson, wrote a letter to Dr. Leon Ransom, Pauli's mentor and the advisor to the NAACP student chapter, ordering the group to "desist from its program of direct action in the city of Washington." President Johnson had been an outspoken champion of civil rights in churches, on the radio, and in other high-profile places, but when it came to action, he balked. In truth, the university's board members were afraid that Congress, which provided sixty percent of the school's funding, would withhold its financial support of Howard.

Though short-lived and only partly successful, the direct actions at the Little Palace Cafeteria and Thompson's Restaurant were the first sit-ins staged at segregated restaurants in the United States. Not until nineteen years later, in 1963, would another group of brave college students try the tactic again, at a Woolworths lunch counter in Greensboro, North Carolina.

Wondering how to attack the customary segregation in the nation's capital from another angle, Pauli and a few senior law students were discussing the issue when Professor H. Mercer Daniel, the oldest member of the law school's faculty, mentioned he'd heard talk of a civil rights law in the District of Columbia. "Poppa" Daniel was a painstaking researcher who found the statute in a document called, "Compiled Statutes in Force in the District of Columbia in 1894."

In 1872, an act was passed by the Second Legislature Assembly of the District of Columbia that made it a misdemeanor "punishable by a fine of $100 and forfeiture of a restaurant license for one year for proprietors of restaurants, ice cream saloons, soda fountains, hotels, barbershops, and bathing houses" to refuse to serve "any respectable, well-behaved person without regard to race, color, or previous condition of servitude . . . in the same room, and at the same prices as other well-behaved and respectable persons are served."

Pauli and other committed students pored over the books in the law library late into the night until their eyes glazed over, searching for a repeal of that law, since the law was clearly not being enforced. The statute did not appear in any book of the Code of Laws since 1884. But neither was there any repeal of the statute. There was no citation that it had been declared invalid by judicial decision. Finally, Pauli stumbled over an esoteric 1901 code of the District of Columbia.

"Look at this," Pauli exclaimed to the stares of other students. "It says right here that 'all laws herein before enacted, but not expressly repealed, are held to be in full force and effect.' That means the Act of 1872 is still in effect."

"But, remember," a friend said, "the Supreme Court invalidated the federal Civil Rights Act of 1875 in the decision on the Civil Rights Cases of 1883. But did that invalidate this Act of 1872?"

"We should bring a test case of this," Pauli said, looking around at her friends huddled over the ancient law book.

"Pauli, you're about to graduate; you won't have time to make a formal legal memorandum," one friend said.

"It would be too expensive to run the costly litigation at this time," another said. "Besides, we are working on more pressing matters than accommodations at local establishments, such as fair trials and voting rights."

They had to wait until five years later, when Mary Church Terrell chaired the Coordinating Committee for the Enforcement of DC Anti-Discrimination Laws, to see segregation tested in court. The test case happened in 1950 against their old nemesis—Thompson's Cafeteria—when Terrell tried again to be served. The case reached the Supreme Court in the spring of 1953, three months before Mrs. Terrell's ninetieth birthday, and was decided in favor of upholding the 1872 law to prohibit segregation of public facilities in the District of Columbia, since it had never been repealed.

In 1944, Pauli spoke to her graduating class at Howard. "Can we attract young White graduates of the great universities up North to come down and join with us? I say we can. And I'll say this too—we spend all of our time fighting against the separate but equal provisions of the Plessy vs. Ferguson case. Most of the cases concentrate on showing that the separate facilities are not equal on a case-by-case basis. But we need to attack the problem head on, not in this piecemeal fashion. I recommend that we challenge the notion that separate can ever be equal. That separate status in and of itself implies inferiority."

Dr. Ransom came up to her afterward with Professor Spottswood. Dr. Ransom said, "Professor Spottswood and I will bet you ten dollars, Miss Murray, that Plessy vs Ferguson will be overturned in twenty-five years."

"Oh, Dr. Ransom, I do hope it will come faster than that. If we put forth this argument, it surely will."

In fact, the argument set forth by Pauli Murray was the argument used in Brown vs. Board of Education, which stated that separate schools were inherently unequal. And it came not twenty-five years later but within ten years!

Dean William Hastie asked Pauli what she intended to do after graduation.

"Why, I don't know, sir. I have been so involved in all these civil rights actions, I've only been concentrating on making it to graduation, hopefully with a *cum laude* degree."

"Why don't you think about getting a masters in law and coming back here to teach? The faculty would be glad to have you."

"I would very much like to continue my studies in the area of labor law."

"Well, you should apply for the Rosenwald Fellowship."

Pauli mentioned the idea to some of her classmates. "I suppose I shall have to apply to Harvard. That's where half the Howard faculty received their advanced degrees."

"Harvard? Where have you been, girl? You'll never get in there. You want to know why?" The young men looked at each other, grinning.

Pauli stiffened. "Why?"

"Because they don't accept women!" And the men all joined in a good laugh.

Pauli's struggles as a woman at Howard and the disappointment she suffered about Harvard not admitting women marked the beginning of her sense that civil rights was also a gender issue.

"Someday, we'll be working to strike down 'Jane Crow' laws as well as Jim Crow injustices," she told her students, coining a phrase she would later use in a 1965 article titled, "Jane Crow and the Law." Still, she wasn't going to let anything ruin the great joy she and her family shared upon attending her graduation in Washington in the spring of 1944.

A high point of the event was when a huge bouquet of roses was delivered to the school a half hour before the ceremony. Pauli noticed them in the hallway when she came to pick up her cap and gown.

"Oh, how beautiful these are," she said to her friend Ruth Powell as she bent over to smell them. "They must be for Dr. Charlotte Hawkins Brown who is receiving an honorary degree today."

"No, they aren't, silly," exclaimed Ruth. "You ought to read the card, dear."

Pauli opened the card and read the congratulatory note "to Miss Pauli Murray from her friend, Eleanor Roosevelt."

"Oh, my," said Pauli. "Oh, my," she repeated. "How very sweet of the First Lady to remember me. But I really must share this with all the graduates." She called to the secretary of the law school as he passed by. "Mr. Nabrit, couldn't we bring these flowers into the hall so everyone can see them. They should be for everyone."

And so, Mr. Nabrit carried the bright red bouquet across the wide lawn while the students were lining up for the procession, and placed them on the platform where the students were to receive their degrees.

The next day, Pauli brought the flowers to the Church of the Atonement in Washington, DC, where she and her aunts attended the Sunday service. Afterward, Pauli requested that they be taken to the Freedman's Hospital so their beauty could brighten the hours of the sick and bedridden. Before she let the bouquet go, Pauli pulled the purple satin ribbon from around the vase and placed it in her Bible, where it remained all her life, a cherished token of a special friendship.

Chapter 16

Proud Shoes

After being rejected by Harvard for a post-doctorate, which would enable her to teach law, Pauli was accepted at Boalt Hall School of Jurisprudence in Berkeley, California. From there, she was appointed to a temporary position as deputy attorney general of California, the first African American and first woman to hold this position. Unfortunately, she was again called back from California to care for her adoptive mother. She took a temporary leave of absence to return to North Carolina, but by the time she had transferred Aunt Pauline to Freedman's Hospital in Washington, DC, where she was finally diagnosed with diabetes and was on her way to recovery, Pauli had lost the opportunity to apply for the permanent position as deputy attorney general.

For the next few years she had a difficult time gaining her footing and making a living as a lawyer. She was a legal research assistant at a Jewish organization, a law clerk for an African American lawyer in Brooklyn, and even struck out on her own after passing the New York bar. But, not having access to wealthy clients, she was never able to fully support herself with independent legal work. Even so, she was able to provide a home for her two aging aunts who had now come to live with her in her three-room, second-floor walk-up in Brooklyn.

The Fitzgerald family had finally sold Grandmother Cornelia's farm, which she'd inherited from her former White mistress, so the two single women had a little extra money to retire on.

At least the various jobs Pauli held during these years provided her with health insurance, which she didn't have while in California. Before Pauli had driven out West with her sister Mildred, she'd consulted with a doctor in New York about the possibility of being injected with male hormones. She was still concerned about her sexuality. Rather than aiming to become more feminine, she wished to become more masculine, although she probably did not intend to completely change her identity and present herself as a male. Mildred, who was a nurse, had accepted a better job at the Veterans Hospital in Los Angeles and Pauli assumed she would be able to administer the testosterone injections during their cross-country drive. But Mildred had always disapproved of Pauli's "boy-girl personality," and neglected to arrange anything with Pauli's doctor.

At Boalt Hall, Pauli experienced abdominal pain caused by a displaced uterus. The condition wasn't life-threatening, so she decided to postpone surgery until she had insurance. She took the opportunity to write the doctor who had prescribed the hormone treatments, asking whether doctors could look for anything physically unusual when she elected to have the surgery. Before her second year at Howard, Pauli finally persuaded Dr. Chinn to perform an x-ray on her reproductive organs to see if there was something different about her.

"Dr. Chinn, I'm convinced my nervous condition and dissatisfaction with my gender is more physical than psychological. I wish you would look into the possibility that it could be a glandular disturbance. Or maybe I don't have enough female hormones, which is causing my apparent virility. Or could there be male organs hidden in my abdomen?"

Dr. Chinn came back with the x-ray report and sat down with Pauli with the patience she had grown used to employing with her difficult client.

"The x-ray shows that your fallopian tubes are normal, your uterus is small and malpositioned, which is normal, and you most likely have an excess of female hormones, not a lack of them. Your reproductive organs are normal, Pauli, and there is no sign of any secondary sex characteristics."

Pauli couldn't do anything but accept this conclusion, but years later, after she returned from California, she hadn't given up on her quest for a physiological answer to her conflict.

When she could no longer bear the abdominal pain that had been bothering her off and on for a year and a half, Pauli submitted to exploratory surgery at Sydenham Hospital in Harlem to see about her malpositioned uterus. She asked the doctor to investigate whether she might have pseudo-hermaphroditism or hidden male genitals, but he only found an infected appendix and two infected fallopian tubes, which he removed. Pauli's sexual conflicts may have been unresolved, but she was finally able to move on from attributing them to a purely physical condition. At age thirty-seven, Pauli had more hurdles ahead of her, but she would also be involved in a remarkable array of achievements that would change the cultural and political norms of American life in the last half of the twentieth century.

In 1952, Pauli applied for a job as research assistant to the director of codification of laws of Liberia at Cornell. The university asked her to submit supplemental background information about organizations she had belonged to in the past. The hiring committee found that she had worked for the travel agency that organized tours to the Soviet Union, which gave them cause to doubt her loyalty to the United States. In the mistrustful anti-communist climate instigated by Wisconsin Senator Joseph McCarthy, the college rejected her application.

The application committee informed her that "there were some questions concerning her past associations," which they felt "might place the university in a difficult situation." This phrase, "past associations," seemed to malign all of Pauli's ancestors and the illustrious people she had come to know on her journey to secure the civil rights and decency her people deserved. She had submitted references from many illustrious people: her mentor at Howard Law School, Judge William H. Hastie, who sat on the bench of the US Court of Appeals; labor leader A. Philip Randolph, head of the Pullman Porters Union; Lloyd K. Garrison, descendent of abolitionist Lloyd Garrison; future supreme court justice Thurgood Marshall; and finally, former First Lady Eleanor Roosevelt.

She told the admissions director, "I'm sorry if I don't know anyone of more 'conservative' persuasion who is well enough acquainted with me to give an informed opinion. If *their* judgment is questionable, then there is no one who could vouch for my loyalty."

It was the phrase, 'past associations,' that motivated Pauli to sit down at her twenty-year-old typewriter and write the following words:

"If Grandfather Robert George Fitzgerald had not volunteered for the Union forces in 1863, and come South three years later as a missionary among the Negro freedmen, our family might not have walked in such proud shoes and felt so assured of its official place in American history. We might have fought our battles with poverty and color troubles, thinking of ourselves as nobodies or not thinking of ourselves at all, and died out with nothing to remember about us except a few census figures."

Pauli remembered how the poet Stephen Vincent Benét had encouraged her to write about her family's history, and she felt she was finally ready to do it. To begin her story and verify her family's legends, Pauli traveled to the National Archives in Washington, DC, to read the United States Census of 1850. She was poring over documents one long afternoon when the woman next to her suddenly jumped up and exclaimed to everyone in the room, "I've found it! I've found it! My ancestor really did shoe horses for soldiers in George

Washington's army during the Revolution. He is listed right here as a blacksmith."

Pauli smiled as she continued the painstaking perusal of pages and pages of census records, searching for her great-grandfather Thomas Fitzgerald's name. She finally found him listed in the 1850 census as a Free Man of Color; profession: farmer; worth: six thousand dollars. And she saw his signature on the deed to his farm in Chester County, Pennsylvania. His property turned out to be very near the entrance to Lincoln University.

Pauli traveled to Lincoln University and met up with a postman-turned-history buff in Chester County. Driving on bumpy, winding dirt roads and hiking through damp woods, he took her on a tour of sites associated with the Underground Railroad. They uncovered boundary stones lost in brambles that informed the fugitives that they had finally reached free soil. They peeked into stone houses and opened doors leading to tunnels where escapees were hidden by sympathetic abolitionists. She saw the site of the Pine Grove schoolhouse where the Fitzgerald children likely attended school.

"What do you think, Mother and Aunt Sallie?" Pauli asked her aunts when she returned home to Brooklyn. "Do you think Great-Grandfather earned that six-thousand dollars by his own efforts or did he receive it in a will from our mysterious Irish ancestor?"

"I don't believe anyone in this family ever received any gifts from anyone," Aunt Sallie insisted.

"I'll have to go down to the county courthouse in Wilmington, Delaware, to find out," Pauli said.

That was how, one quiet afternoon, sitting at a table in the dusty records room of the Wilmington County Courthouse with a box of records in front of her, Pauli found something that no one in her family would have expected—a duly recorded deed to Thomas Fitzgerald, dated August 8, 1832, that read as follows:

"I, George Lodge, for divers reasons and considerations have manumitted, discharged and forever set free from servitude of myself, my heirs, executors, administrators from and after this date hereof, a certain Coloured man named Thomas Fitsgirls, aged twenty-four years and eight days old who fell to me by will of my father, Samuel Lodge."

Pauli's breath came up short. She looked up from the papers and looked around the room as if seeking guidance, but there was no one else in the hushed room. She was having a difficult time believing what she had read. Her family had always gained strength from the belief that, at least on their Fitzgerald side, their ancestors had not been enslaved. Now she saw how untrue, how naïve and unrealistic, that notion was.

After taking in this momentous information, Pauli continued looking further into the history of the Lodge family. She found they were Quakers whose only bonded people were house servants whom they listed in the census as free people of color living in their households. Thomas came into the family when he was eleven years old. It was George Lodge who most likely taught him to read and write. As was the Quaker custom, all their servants were freed upon reaching the age of twenty-four.

Pauli continued working on her book and was sometimes able to break away from her law practice with the help of writing fellowships. In 1954, she received a grant to spend the summer at the MacDowell artists' residency in New Hampshire, where she and James Baldwin were the first Black writers admitted.

The next year, Aunt Pauline celebrated her eighty-fifth birthday on September 25, 1955, remarking that she was pleased she had surpassed the age of the family's longest surviving relative, Great-Aunt Mary Jane Fitzgerald. The night of October 25, the venerable lady had a massive heart attack. It was before dawn. Pauli finally got in touch with the night physician at her own doctor's office, and he came for a house call first thing in the morning.

"She needs to go to the hospital as soon as possible," the doctor told Pauli. "I've given her some medication. She may be having trouble with her gall bladder, or it may be her heart. Which hospital is her doctor affiliated with?"

"Saint John's."

"I'll call them, but they probably won't admit her until she is referred by her own doctor."

Finally, Aunt Pauline's doctor came midmorning to make arrangements with the hospital. An ambulance was scheduled to arrive in the afternoon.

Pauline whispered in her weakened voice, "Pauli, I don't think I'll live to get to the hospital. I've got death rattles in my throat." Pauli tried to reach the reverend at St. Philip's church to administer Holy Communion, but he was not available.

Pauli pulled her chair closer to her aunt and held her hand. "Would you like me to read the "Order for the Visitation of the Sick" from the *Book of Common Prayer*?"

Pauline nodded weakly.

Pauli remembered that it was always the eldest in their family who conducted the prayers and the reading of the Bible. Pauli had never taken on the reading herself. She felt unworthy of participating in this hallowed ritual. It was her first experience ministering to a dying person. She did not know then that this would be a life-changing experience for her, to offer ministry to the dying. She read the words from the *Book of Common Prayer*:

Pauline Fitzgerald Dame.

Keep her in perpetual peace and safety . . .

Grant her an abiding sense of thy loving-kindness.

Unto God's gracious mercy and protection we commit thee.

In the next moment, Aunt Pauline took her last breath and left this world.

Pauli continued feverishly writing the history of her family, which she intended to call *Proud Shoes*. She needed to finish it soon, because she was running out of money. Aunt Sallie seemed to have lost the will to keep on after her older sister and lifelong companion died. Ultimately, she stopped eating. When Pauli offered to call the doctor, she said, "Why call the doctor? I haven't seen a doctor in thirty-seven years." When she finally allowed a doctor to see her, he diagnosed her illness as cancer of the liver.

Pauli understood that all she could do was be with her aunt, to comfort her in her last days. Sallie waited until *Proud Shoes* was published, then died two days later. Again, a celebration was mixed with sadness in Pauli's life.

*Pauli Murray with Lloyd K. Garrison (2nd from left) on the date of publication of **Proud Shoes**, 1956.*

Chapter 17

Hyde Park

While she was writing *Proud Shoes*, Pauli was sometimes diverted by invitations to visit Mrs. Roosevelt. They were usually personal visits squeezed in between the former First Lady's many important commitments. But sometimes Pauli found herself at the table with illustrious world figures. Once, she sat at lunch next to Andrei Gromyko, the Soviet delegate to the United Nations. It was such an honor to be in Eleanor's presence, Pauli often arranged for a friend or relative to accompany her, so they could share some of the excitement.

After her niece, Bonnie, graduated from Catholic University in 1954, Pauli took her aside and asked, "How would you like to come with me to Hyde Park? Mrs. Roosevelt invited me to her estate on the Hudson River. Wouldn't that be a nice graduation present?

"Oh, Pauli, you know it would," Bonnie enthused. "I've wanted to meet her ever since you took Great Aunt Pauline and my mother to her apartment for tea ten years ago. After all, I was born the month President Roosevelt first started his terms in office, and you still wouldn't let me go!"

"But you were only eleven years old then. Now you are quite old enough."

Bonnie took the train to New York and they hailed a cab to Mrs. Roosevelt's apartment downtown. As they stood outside, chatting with the doorman, waiting for her to come down, gusts of wind made their coats fly up.

"Pauli, isn't Hurricane Hazel due to strike this evening? Are you sure this is the best time?" Bonnie asked.

"As long as Mrs. R is game, we'll be ready," Pauli said.

The car came around and Mrs. Roosevelt took the front seat next to her chauffeur.

"Mr. White," said Pauli, leaning forward to speak to the driver, "I was just telling my niece Bonnie that the wonderful singer, Josh White, is your brother. Do you also have a talent for singing?"

"Oh my, no," said Mr. White. "I do all my singing in church, hoping my faulty baritone will mix in with the heavenly choir. But I might have to start singing special praises to the Lord right now to spare us from the might of this Hurricane Hazel."

"You might step on the gas a little more, Mr. White," said Mrs. Roosevelt. "I'm hoping we can beat this windy lady going north. And if you don't mind, I'm going to take this opportunity to catch a few winks."

The winds picked up in strength as they drove north up the Hudson River Parkway. The trees along the roadside swayed wildly. Severed branches and leaves were scattered on the road in front of them and falling twigs occasionally obscured the windshield. When they came up the driveway of Mrs. Roosevelt's cottage on the grounds of Hyde Park, they could see that the house was in total darkness.

"My goodness," said Mrs. Roosevelt. "The storm must have knocked out the electricity."

Using a flashlight from the car, Mrs. Roosevelt made her way into the house and down the hall into the kitchen, where she went straight for a drawer that stored candles and matchsticks. She quickly lit a candle and placed it on a holder, and guided her guests upstairs to their rooms. They had no sooner entered their quaint white room with the bedspreads opened invitingly when Mrs. Roosevelt said, "Hurry up, girls, and put down your bags. There isn't time to unpack. We have an engagement at Bard College and we don't want to keep the girls waiting."

"You have an engagement tonight, Mrs. Roosevelt?" Bonnie asked, dismayed.

"I'm to read the students a bedtime story," the elder woman laughed. "Not really—I am going to read selections from

Pauli's niece, Bonnie Fearing, around 1946.

T.S. Eliot and James Stephens, then wind it up with *Winnie-the-Pooh*."

"Don't you think the students will understand if you can't keep the appointment in the middle of a hurricane?" Pauli pressed.

"Well, I'm also to have dinner with the president of the college and his wife. I suppose *they* would understand, but I don't think I can let down the students."

"Are we going to have time to change for dinner?"

"Oh, no, no. Don't worry about that. I just hope we make it in *time* for dinner."

They bustled back into the roadster and braved the twenty miles to the college, passing dangerously swollen streams along the way. They were only a short distance from the entrance to the campus when Mr. White encountered a huge tree that had been uprooted and was lying across the road.

"Well," said Mrs. Roosevelt, "we'll just have to get out and walk the

Pauli Murray with Eleanor Roosevelt at Valkill Cottage, Hyde Park, NY.

rest of the way. How fortunate that we are almost there."

As they approached a large building, Mrs. Roosevelt said, "That's the hall where I'm supposed to read. Let's go there first, since we're so late."

A student opened the door, astonished to see the bedraggled group. "Why, Mrs. Roosevelt, we had long ago given up hope that you would come."

"Well, we're here, just in time for the reading as I promised," said Mrs. Roosevelt a little sternly.

"But you've missed dinner!"

"Oh, never mind that. Let's get to the business at hand."

All the students lucky enough to be selected for the reading gathered around a crackling fire in the large common room. Mrs. Roosevelt delighted them with her dramatic flair. Only after she finished with *Winnie-the-Pooh* were sandwiches and cups of hot coffee brought in to see the travelers through on the drive home. Hurricane Hazel had pushed farther north, leaving only a steady downpour. The electricity was still out in the cottage at Hyde Park, so they kept on using the candles. As they settled under the warm quilts, Pauli and Bonnie heard Mrs. Roosevelt calling cheerfully from down the hall, "Breakfast at nine, girls!"

Pauli awoke about 8 a.m. and switched on the lamp to see if the electricity was back. It wasn't.

"I don't know if I can get through this morning without a good strong cup of coffee," Pauli lamented to Bonnie in the bed next to her.

"I don't think I can get out of this wonderfully warm bed," murmured Bonnie.

In a moment they were startled by a knock on the door. Mrs. Roosevelt appeared in a white terrycloth bathrobe. Her head was encased in a turbaned towel and her cheeks were ruddy, as though they'd had a good scrubbing.

"I've just had my morning bath, girls. I'll tell you what you can do, since there isn't any hot water in the house—there is a swimming pool around by my brother-in-law John's house and nobody uses it this time of year. I just came back from a lovely dip. I took my soap and towel down with me, looked up and down the road to see that nobody was coming, then rubbed myself all over with soap, stepped right down into the pool, and took my bath. If you hurry, you can do the same. Just be sure nobody's looking from the house. See you later." With that, she drew back her head and closed the door.

Pauli laughed. "What do you say, Bonnie? Shall we rise to the challenge?"

Bonnie looked at Pauli in disbelief. "She's more eccentric than I thought. It's October, Pauli. We've just had a storm. She's seventy years old! She could have lost her balance on her way into the pool."

"Mrs. R? Not likely."

The two women put on their bathrobes and ventured outside, carrying their soap and towels with them. Looking both ways, they made their way across the wide expanse of lawn in front of John Roosevelt's house. As they walked by the back door, John's wife, Anne, opened the door and stared at the two women, wondering what intruders had made their way onto the grounds.

"Um, we were looking for the pool?" Pauli stammered.

"Are you with Eleanor?"

"Yes, ma'am."

"But you *can't* take a swim in the pool this time of the year."

"Mrs. Roosevelt just finished taking her bath there, and she suggested we do the same."

"Oh, that Eleanor, up to her old tricks. What are we going to do with her? But if that's what you want to do, I will show you where it is." She pointed the way and was about to go back in the house when she turned. "Mind, I've sent for a truck to bring several milk cans of water. It will be here soon."

The pool was right next to the main driveway. And sure enough, they saw the truck arriving. They waited until the driver had carted the big cans of water up to the house. Then a huge St. Bernard rounded the corner of the house and took a leisurely walk around the pool, stopping to lap the water at the shallow end. After the truck passed, they stepped into the water only knee high, keeping their undergarments on, and made a rather cursory attempt at washing. Then they hurried back to the cottage only to find that the electricity was back on again and the smell of coffee was already wafting from the kitchen.

They lunched that day up at John and Anne's house. Mrs. Roosevelt's seven-year-old granddaughter started the conversation. "Mama, I saw Grandmére take off her robe and go down the steps into the pool this morning."

"And *I* encountered two complete strangers at my backdoor asking me to point them the way to the pool," her mother answered.

Mrs. Roosevelt, unruffled, added her part. "There must have been a swimming meet

Aunt Pauline and Aunt Sallie at Valkill Cottage with Eleanor Roosevelt.

going on down there."

Pauli would always remember how Mrs. Roosevelt lit the candles so efficiently in the dark when she discovered they were without electricity. It seemed fitting that, after she died, her epitaph read "Lighting a Candle in the Darkness."

Chapter 18

Ghana

For three years, Pauli worked in the law offices of Paul, Weiss, Rifkind, Wharton & Garrison. The grandson of abolitionist William Lloyd Garrison had encouraged her to apply for this job after she'd worked with him on a civil rights case. At the law office, she worked on business law, corporate mergers, and tax cases.

At age forty-six, Pauli had to adjust to working with young White attorneys, most of them with law degrees from Harvard and Yale. She was one of three women attorneys in the office and the only African American. Fortunately, the office manager, Irene Barlow, was a plucky woman who took Pauli under her wing.

Irene was a White woman, also in her forties, who had pulled herself up by her bootstraps as a poor immigrant from Yorkshire, England. After Irene's father abandoned the family, her mother scraped up the money to bring her five children to America. They were stuck on Ellis Island for weeks until they could find a distant relative to vouch for them. The family ended up in New England where the older daughters found work in the textile mills. Irene managed to work her way through high school and two years of college before taking advantage of a good-paying job in the personnel office of a shipbuilding firm in Rhode Island during WWII. That experience led to her position at the prestigious law firm in New York, where she was able to finish her education.

Even though the attorneys were all White men, Irene made it a point to hire a diverse group of staff members. She was sensitive enough to pair Pauli, the new hire, with mentors she would be comfortable with. Stephen Wise Tulin was a Jewish attorney whose grandfather had been a founder of the American Jewish Congress as well as the NAACP, and whose mother was the first female judge in New York. Pauli's secretary was Rosemary Iwami, whose Japanese American family had been interned in a camp during the war.

Another colleague of Pauli's at the Paul, Weiss law firm was a young woman named Ruth Bader Ginsburg, who was working as a summer associate. Although most associates were hired after they completed law school, Ginsburg was turned down because she was a wife and mother. But Ginsburg and Murray would join forces again later on to win a landmark women's rights case.

Pauli and Irene, who went by "Renee" (pronounced Ree-knee), became friends after Renee took Pauli to lunch to help her smooth out some of her rough edges.

"Miss Murray, if you don't want to be hitting some brick walls, you may have to learn to be more diplomatic, and perhaps a bit more graceful in your speech and dress."

"Oh, dear, I hardly know where to start with my clothes!"

"My mother is a great seamstress. She can sew you up some new frocks. We have to turn you into less of a rough diamond and more of the sophisticate."

"I wish I could be more like you. You are so good-humored, with your witty comments. You are always putting out fires and helping all the difficult personalities at the firm get along."

Pauli was frustrated with the piecemeal kind of work she was asked to do. Because it was such a large firm, she was never involved in a case from beginning to end but researched only a small part of each case. She complained to Renee, "I sometimes feel as though I am working on an assembly line. When I had my own practice, I did everything from making copies of depositions to arguing in court."

"Well, at least you don't have to worry about not getting paid," Renee smiled.

The two women discovered a spiritual bond when Renee made a reference to "the blessed company of all faithful people."

"That's from the *Book of Common Prayer*," Pauli remarked. "Does that mean you are an Episcopalian?"

"Why, yes. And you also?"

"Since the day I was born," Pauli answered.

After dropping in on Lenten services during their lunch hour, they eventually started attending St. Mark's Church in-the-Bowery together every Sunday. Their lives were similar in that Renee lived with her aging mother, as Pauli had lived with her aunts. Over time, they became lovers and enjoyed taking vacations together in the Caribbean, though they never lived together and Pauli often pursued her dreams away from New York City.

It was probably her relationship with Renee that encouraged Pauli to stay with the firm for three years. Still, when the practice of law became too routine for this trail-blazing woman who was usually at the forefront of activist causes, she began to hunger for work that was more meaningful. When she saw that a new law school was forming at the University of Accra in Ghana, West Africa, and that they were looking for faculty, she jumped at the prospect, and secured a position teaching constitutional law.

In 1960, she boarded a Norwegian cargo ship, the *SS Tatra*, with her dog Smokey, wondering if she had made the right decision to travel to a foreign country all by herself. The ship stopped for half a day in Halifax, Nova Scotia, and she found a little church by the docks where Sunday service was in progress. The simple liturgy and quaintness of the little church made her homesick for her aunts and for Renee. "Why am I always moving on from wherever I am?" she wondered as tears welled up inside her. She remembered what

Renee had told her as she gave her a last hug goodbye.

"Pauli, you and I have a partnership. We mesh when necessary and disengage when it is no longer necessary. You are embarking on another journey in your spiritual quest for your roots. I'll be here when you return."

Soon Pauli came to love the smell of the salt spray, the wide expanse of ocean and sky, and was curious about the mechanical workings of the ship. The captain showed her all around the ship, down to the bowels of the engine room where they could barely hear themselves speak above the growling of the engine. She stood with the helmsman in the wheelhouse. She learned how to read charts in the chart room, and checked the provisions on the lifeboats.

At dinner, when she sat at the captain's table, Captain Bye said, "Miss Murray knows more about this boat right now than I do. If something happens to us, you don't have to worry, she can take over and run the ship."

"You mean, you would entrust the ship to a woman?" Pauli countered.

"Why, sure. Almost half the radio operators in our shipping line are women. They started during the war and we didn't want to send them back home after it was done. We have a woman engineer on one of our ships. She puts on dungarees and slops about in the engine room supervising the men. I saw a female first mate on a Russian ship—they're much more advanced than Westerners in the area of women's equality."

Pauli was picked up at the airport by a friendly White couple from England. Pauli climbed into Mr. and Mrs. Lang's large station wagon and watched in fascination as they drove through the lush tropical plants on either side of the highway. She saw the streams of citizens riding bikes and walking, many of the women balancing large, gaily painted tin bowls of produce and huge bundles of firewood on their heads. Meanwhile, her hosts were introducing her to the practical matters of starting a household.

"Of course, you'll have to get yourself a houseboy," Mrs. Lang announced.

"A houseboy? You're not serious."

"Of course I am. You need a young male servant to do your cooking and shopping for food. Especially for a woman alone, a houseboy would provide protection too."

"I've never employed anyone to do my household chores. It's against everything I believe, to expect someone else to do that kind of work for me."

"It is part of the economy here, dear. It's an important part of their livelihood. Most people have three servants—a garden boy, a small boy to do the housework, and a head boy to oversee them," said Mrs. Lang.

"And these boys you refer to, they are undoubtedly grown men."

Mrs. Lang looked at her as if there was no need to say the obvious.

As Pauli settled in, numerous Ghanaian men came to apply for various positions.

"I will do your laundry, Miss."

"I will hoe your garden."

"You will need a 'watchnights' to watch over your place. There are too many thieves about, Mistress."

Finally, Pauli gave in and selected a tall young man who had a dignified manner. He was barefoot, but wore a clean shirt and khaki shorts. He showed her the registration papers that allowed him to live in the city away from his home village, unfolding the worn, wrinkled paper so she could see it. On another sheet of paper were his references from previous employers.

Pauli regarded him sternly. "I'm not going to be locking everything up in the house. If you work for me, we will have to trust one another.

Do you understand?"

"If you no trust me, I no trust you," the young man replied.

Pauli read the employment form. "Your name is Yaro Fra Fra?"

"Yes, ma'am. My people are the Fra Fra. Everyone calls me Yaro, ma'am."

One evening, after they felt more comfortable together, Pauli came into the kitchen while Yaro sliced goat meat and onions for cooking. "Yaro, I see

Yaredi Akare, left, Pauli's housekeeper in Accra, Ghana, 1960.

the marks on your face. What does that signify?"

"It is the mark of my tribe, Mistress. That is how we can know our Fra Fra brothers when we are traveling."

"How long has that been a custom?"

"Only since the time of slavery. In those days, parents cut marks on the faces of their babies because it was said that the White slave merchants didn't want people with wounds or disfigurements. Later, it evolved that each group made their markings in a certain way, to identify themselves as part of a particular group."

Pauli thought back to her visit to Elmina Castle on the coast outside of Accra. The slave-trading fort built by the Portuguese in 1481 was used to hold Africans captured in tribal wars who were then sold to Europeans before being put on ships bound for the New World. Knowing that her own grandmother was born a slave made Pauli shiver with unease.

When Pauli discovered Yaro couldn't read, that went against everything she was raised to believe and she had to do something about it. She offered to increase his salary if he would take an adult literacy course in the afternoons. Soon Yaro was writing words on little pieces of paper and placing them on objects around the house. He searched for the words he knew in magazines she left out on the table. Later, he started to write out his grocery list.

He brought his friends and their wives around to introduce them to his employer. Pauli asked him, after seeing the men with their women, "Don't you have a wife, too, Yaro?"

"I do, Miss Pauli. I have a wife, a daughter, and a baby back home. But I cannot bring them here until I pay off the debt I owe to my father-in-law for my bride price."

"How much do you owe?"

"I owe him the price of three cows, and I have paid for only one. If I don't pay it soon, he will take her back and marry her to another man who can pay it."

"Even with your children?"

"Yes."

"Then you must go and get them," Pauli said immediately. She thought about his predicament. "How about if I give you the money for the bride price now, and then I will take an amount out of your salary every week until you have paid me back? I will give you two weeks off to go and pay off your debt."

"Miss Pauli," said Yaro, vigorously shaking her hand, "I will work twice as hard for you when I return."

The Langs were shocked when they heard of Pauli's generosity. "That's the last you'll see of that one, I'm afraid," clucked Mrs. Lang.

Two and a half weeks went by and Yaro did not return. Pauli began to think Mrs. Lang was right. One evening, as she sat out on her veranda, she looked up from her reading and saw a small band of people walking down the road, slowly making their way toward her house. There was a man with a shaved head on which he carried a large bundle of firewood, a woman behind him with a baby wrapped in colorful cloth on her back, a little girl carrying a sack that almost touched the ground, and a boy of about ten pulling along a goat on a leash.

When they neared the house, Pauli recognized the bald man as Yaro.

"We have returned, Miss Pauli," said Yaro, coming in the gate with his entourage behind him. "Here is my wife, Abena, and my daughter, Adjua. And I am your servant, Yaredi Akare."

"Yaredi Akare?"

"Yes, ma'am. That is my true name. I tell it only to those I respect greatly."

"Thank you, Mr. Akare. It is an honor to meet your family. But you have not introduced everyone," said Pauli nodding toward the boy and his goat.

"This is my brother's son, Kofie. My brother has died and I must care for his son. You will notice my head is shaved in mourning for my brother's death."

Yaredi, known as Yaro, took his family to the little one-room bungalow at the end of the garden, where he had been staying. From then on, until Pauli left Ghana, that was where they all lived.

Pauli enjoyed teaching constitutional law at the University of Accra. When Judge William Hastie came for a visit and sat in on one of her classes, he was surprised to hear the students come up with an original line of reasoning on a case, and he complimented Pauli on her excellent teaching. He also praised the brightness of her students.

But perhaps their interpretation of the laws was becoming too sophisticated. As the current president, Kwame Nkrumah, consolidated his power, the government was beginning to monitor professors at the university for signs of dissent. One morning Pauli entered her classroom and found six men in uniforms bearing the insignia of the Criminal Investigation Department sitting in the back of the room. She conducted her class as usual and nothing came of it, but an American professor warned her that living in Ghana was becoming more dangerous for Americans who were considered "stooges of US imperialism."

"Have you considered getting a doctorate in law, Miss Murray?" Professor Harper asked. "Yale has a very good graduate program, and I believe they would be delighted to have such an accomplished lawyer within their ranks."

Pauli remembered the words of her Aunt Sallie: "Sometimes, when one door is closed against us in life, God opens up another door to a greater opportunity." After an exciting and rewarding two years, it was time for Pauli to return to the States.

A group of Ghanaians and Americans.
Pauli is third from right in back row, 1960.

Chapter 19

NOW

Pauli entered the PhD program at Yale Law School in the fall of 1961, and became the first African American to complete a Doctor of Juridical Science at Yale, in 1965, when she was fifty-five years old. She was grateful that New Haven was close to New York City and that she and Renee could easily take the train to visit each other on weekends, but she suffered an all too familiar setback when she tried to find housing near the campus. Friends had introduced her to a member of an interracial committee at the school who offered to take her to a rental office where the owner was a friend of her family. The rental agent took one look at Pauli and turned her down.

"I have nothing against you personally," he sheepishly informed her, "but I simply cannot risk renting an apartment to a Colored person."

Pauli's friend was mortified. To her credit, she filed a complaint against the man with the local antidiscrimination agency. But, for Pauli, the insult and injustice ignited a deep sense of rage.

She wrote to Renee:

> *One is never really prepared for these sudden, ruthless*
> *psychic blows, which, though rendered without physical*

violence, are no less in violation of what is sacred to the
individual—human dignity. The invisible wounds from
racial indignities generate an inner rage which festers
under the surface, often unrelieved until it explodes in
indiscriminate violence against White people.

In response to the acceleration of the civil rights movement, Pauli changed her dissertation from the "Study of Constitutional Rights in New African States" to "The Roots of the Racial Crisis in America: Prologue to Policy." Pauli also closely observed the development of the women's movement. When women began pressing harder for an Equal Rights Amendment for women (first introduced in Congress in 1923), President John Kennedy, issuing an executive order, created the President's Commission on the Status of Women in 1961 to appease them.

The strategy was similar to President Roosevelt's creation of the Fair Employment Practices Committee in 1941 as a response to A. Philip Randolph's threat to march a hundred thousand strong on Washington to press for better working conditions for Black Americans. President Kennedy appointed the elder stateswoman, Eleanor Roosevelt, to chair the commission, which would study "the barriers to full realization of women's basic rights" and "make recommendations for constructive action."

Pauli was invited to serve on the Committee on Civil Rights and Political Rights. The committee issued a report stating that the Constitution's Fourteenth Amendment could apply to equality for women, but specific cases would have to be upheld by the Supreme Court in order to make the amendment apply to women's rights.

In July of 1965, the Equal Employment Opportunity Commission (EEOC) was created to see that the laws in Title VII of the Civil Rights Act would be enforced. It was chaired by Franklin Roosevelt Jr. who, when faced with dealing with the gender aspect of Title VII, said with exasperation, "The whole issue of sex discrimination is terribly complicated." True to the times, he appointed seven close aides to the commission, all of whom were men. As might be expected, enforcing the rules about discrimination against women was a low priority. The executive director of the EEOC declared that the sex provision of Title VII of the Civil Rights Act was a "fluke." In a way, it was.

Senator Howard Smith of Virginia had actually introduced the word "sex" to Title VII to go along with race, creed, color, or national origin as a way to *prevent* its passage. Smith thought no one would support the Civil Rights bill if it included provisions for women's equality. The strategy didn't work this time—the bill passed in the House by 168 to 133—but when it reached the Senate, Everett Dirksen, the powerful senator from Illinois, quickly introduced an amendment to have the sex discrimination provision taken out.

Pauli had a friend, Catherine East, who worked in the Interdepartmental Committee on the Status of Women at the EEOC. Government employees were not supposed to state their opinions except as citizens, but Catherine worked late at her office compiling information on court actions, administrative decisions, and legislation related to women's rights. She meticulously copied newspaper clippings and legal documents on the new Xerox machine in the Labor Department's office and mailed out informational packets to a growing list of women on their activist mailing list. All of this groundwork would push them forward toward the creation of a national organization devoted to women's rights.

When the women found out that Senator Dirksen was trying to take the word "sex" out of the Senate version of the bill, Catherine immediately called Pauli on the phone, wondering what to do.

"Pauli, how should we proceed? Most of the women, like myself, who even know this is going on are federal employees and not allowed to lobby for a particular position. There isn't time to alert the media and mobilize for popular support. Perhaps you could do something because you do not work for the government."

"The only thing I can do is take pen to paper and lay out our position, and see that it gets to the right people, as I have always done," Pauli answered, a tone of resignation sounding in her voice.

Pauli put together a brief titled: "Memorandum in Support of Retaining the Amendment to PH.R. 7152 (Equal Employment Opportunity) to Prohibit Discrimination in Employment Because of Sex." She argued that if sex discrimination were not retained, there would be no protections for half of the African American population the bill was supposed to protect. The memorandum stated, "there are few, if any, jobs for which an employee's sex could be considered relevant." The memorandum was sent to numerous people including the only female senator, Margaret Chase Smith, who stood up for the amendment on the floor of the Senate and convinced so many Republicans that it should pass, that Senator Dirksen withdrew his objections.

Many worried that Black women would never be able to enjoy the benefits of any gains made by the Civil Rights Act if they were discriminated against as women as well. Pauli co-authored an article that appeared in the *George Washington Law Review* in December 1965, titled "Jane Crow and the Law: Sex Discrimination and Title VII." She argued that "the rights of women and the rights of Negroes are only different phases of the fundamental and indivisible issue of human rights."

In 1969, Ruth Bader Ginsburg came across Murray's article while researching everything she could find about gender discrimination for a case that would overturn an 1864 Idaho law stating that when more than one person was qualified to serve, males must be chosen over females. Ginsburg built on Murray's analysis when writing her groundbreaking Brandeis Brief, which showed how discrimination against women was similar to racial discrimination. So indebted was she for Murray's insight that Ginsburg named Pauli Murray as a co-author of the brief.

The movement for women's rights was entering a new phase in 1965, and Pauli Murray was in the forefront of its legal analysis. She was often called upon to speak on the history and significance of Title VII. On October 12, she spoke at the National Council of Women's Conference at the Biltmore Hotel in New York.

In her speech to mostly White, middle-class women, she warned, "Title VII may not be enforced unless the political power of women is brought to bear. It should not be necessary to have another march on Washington in order that there be equal job opportunities for all. But if this necessity should arise, I hope women will not flinch from the thought."

The next day, the headline in the *New York Times* read, "PROTEST PROPOSED ON WOMEN'S JOBS; YALE PROFESSOR SAYS IT MAY BE NEEDED TO OBTAIN RIGHTS."

Pauli laughed. "And to think, I am just a doctor of law candidate who is being turned down for jobs as a professor because of my sex, or race, or age. If it gives our cause extra clout, let them say what they want. They didn't even mention that I am a Negro. Now, that is a first."

The truth is, Pauli was bitterly disappointed that she had not been offered a teaching position at Yale after graduation. Yet, thirty-six years after her death, in 2017, Yale University would honor Pauli by naming a college after her—the Pauli Murray College—in recognition of her many achievements in furthering human rights.

Now, she was packing up to return to New York when Betty Friedan, the author of *The Feminine Mystique*, which everyone was reading, called Pauli on the telephone after seeing the provocative headline.

"I'd like to interview you for a book I am researching," she said.

"I'd be happy to meet with you," said Pauli. "I have been studying the history of women's rights for some years now. I consider it a natural outgrowth of my involvement in civil rights."

They continued their conversation in Betty Friedan's apartment.

"As a single woman who has to fend for herself, I am acutely aware of the problem. Half the time, I don't know whether I am being discriminated against because of my sex or because of my race," said Pauli.

"At least we have organizations like the National Council for Women that are beginning to address these issues," said Betty.

"But they never quite get there, do they?" Pauli pressed. "And they are still part of the government, which is a slow-moving entity. I have been working with a group of women and we have a mailing list of women who are following these issues and pressing for change any way they can."

"You're telling me about an underground network of women who are poised for action?"

"Exactly," said Pauli. "If only we had a network of about five hundred key women around the country who could spring into action whenever issues directly affecting women arise in Washington."

Both women attended the Third National Conference of State Commissions on the Status of Women. Friedan was there to observe and write on the conference; Murray would be serving on a panel on the last morning of the conference, called "Sex Discrimination – Progress on Legal Status."

On the second day of the conference, they found sympathetic women who were also feeling frustrated by the slow pace of activity. Friedan invited a few of them to her hotel room that evening. At about 10 p.m., fifteen energetic women crowded into the tiny room. At first they vented their anger.

"I agree with Congresswoman Martha Griffith, who spoke on the floor of the House. She said, 'The whole attitude of the EEOC toward discrimination based on sex is specious, negative, and arrogant.'"

"The EEOC has even allowed jobs to continue to be advertised in the newspaper under 'male' and 'female.' If that isn't discrimination, what is?"

"Richard Graham, our only real ally on the Commission, may not be reappointed when his term expires."

"The commission is just dragging its feet on issues of women's equality."

"We need a new organization that isn't part of the government," one woman suggested.

"That will never work," another countered. "We will just be ignored. We already have the National Council of Women. We have more power if we work through the system."

"Look," interrupted Kay Clarenbach, chair of the Wisconsin Commission, "since the theme of this conference is 'target for action,' let's press for a strong resolution at the conference closing. We will call for stronger enforcement of the sex provision of Title VII and the reappointment of Commissioner Graham."

"Kay, you don't really think they will go for that, do you?"

"Even if they do, it will just be words. When they get back to Washington, it will be business as usual. The issues will be 'too complicated.'"

It was already past midnight when Kay went back to her room and put together her resolution.

As Pauli left Betty's room, she paused at the door. "Betty, I am so depressed, I may leave right after my speech on 'Progress in Legal Status.' I thought we were going to get something going here. I feel our dream of starting our own organization has been totally stifled. This conference is where it should have happened."

"Stick around, kid. Sometimes you have to give people a chance to fail. You never know what might happen tomorrow."

Just before her speech, Kay came up to Pauli fuming. "Pauli, Catherine Conway and I talked to the conference officials about introducing our resolution at the final luncheon. They told us flatly no. They confirmed that 'government commissions cannot take action against other departments.'"

Pauli couldn't help smiling. "Are you ready to start a movement?"

"You bet we are," Kay answered.

Pauli didn't know that, during her panel, Kay and Catherine were so upset by the dismissal of their resolution, they were calling together all the women who'd met in Betty Friedan's room. After Pauli's panel, the conference was abuzz with women discussing the need to form a new organization.

Twenty women gathered at two tables in front of the platform where speakers were giving their final speeches to close the conference. They spoke in hushed and angry whispers.

"It's clear we have to form a committee outside of government. They are right when they say that one department can't take an action against another department."

Friedan began scribbling notes on a napkin as the women began to speak aloud and outline their mission. She wrote:

"We must take the actions needed to bring women into the mainstream of American society now . . . in fully equal partnership with men."

"We need a full-fledged organization with dues paying members. And we need it now—N-O-W!"

"What shall we call it?"

"You said it: N-O-W. The National Organization for Women.

Bella Abzug, Donna E. Shalala, and Pauli Murray at Hunter College Inauguration of President, 1980.

What could be better?"

"Perfect! That's perfect." They all joined in a chorus, trying not to call attention to themselves by erupting in joyous solidarity.

After the conference ended, twenty-eight women signed on as founding members, each donating five dollars to get started. They immediately sent a telegram to President Johnson calling for the reappointment of Richard Graham to the EEOC. They wrote to the EEOC calling for the elimination of male and female help wanted ads.

After a summer of planning and organization, thirty-two women met in Washington in October of 1966 to set up a permanent organization. Always ahead of her time, Pauli made sure that the issue of equity was included in NOW's statement of purpose: "We realize that women's problems are linked to many broader questions of social justice." Twenty years later, the National Organization for Women would have more than two hundred thousand members, becoming the largest organization of feminist grassroots activists in the United States.

Chapter 20

A Spiritual Path

Pauli's success in helping to organize NOW made her more keenly sensitive to inequality in other areas of her life. On a cold Sunday in March of 1966, Pauli looked around at the congregation during the performing of the Eucharist at her beloved church, St. Mark's in-the-Bowery. She and Renee had been faithfully attending services there since 1956, when they started going during their lunch hour at the Paul, Weiss law firm. Now, Pauli couldn't help noticing that only the men were wearing the embroidered ivory garments and deep purple gold-edged vestments. Only the men acted as thurifers who could swing the incense, or as crucifers who could carry the cross. Only men served as deacons and subdeacons who could handle the sacred vessels.

Irene Barlow as a young woman.

The only visible presence of women on Sunday was either in the choir or in the pews.

While receiving the wafer and wine from the Reverend Michael Allen, Pauli's face suddenly went flush with a rising sense of injustice. Instead of returning to her seat with the other members of the congregation, she kept walking down the aisle past Renee who looked up in surprise. She stopped on the front steps, pulling her coat around her in the bright sunshine of the crisp spring day. Renee could see her distress and got up to follow her out of the church. She found Pauli doing her usual pacing on the wide steps.

"Come on, let's walk," said Renee, grabbing Pauli's arm and guiding her down the stairs, into the street.

"Renee," Pauli fumed, "I've been taught all my life to revere the church and its teachings, but now I see it as sinful because it denies me the right to participate as fully and freely in the worship of God as my brethren. If these customs are justified, I don't belong in the church. It has become a stumbling block to my faith."

Renee realized how serious Pauli's concerns were. "Did you know, Pauli, that no church laws exist to bar women from functioning as lay readers, acolytes, or from other services? It is only custom that enforces these outdated practices, not the letter of the law. In reality, it is up to the rector to portion out these responsibilities."

"What are you saying? How do you know this?" Pauli stopped her furious pace and stood still, questioning Renee.

"I looked it up in the bylaws," Renee smiled proudly, continuing to walk. "It's not for nothing I've spent my whole career working in law firms."

"Then it is like the segregation laws in the nation's Capital," Pauli insisted. "Not on the books, but just a matter of custom."

"That's right, honey. And just as difficult to crack, I'm sure," Renee laughed.

Pauli wrote a letter of protest to the church vestry, seeking the inclusion of women in liturgical activities. The Reverend Allen immediately called a meeting of interested members to discuss the issue. Many women opposed the idea of being included in more activities of the liturgy.

"I'm a traditionalist," said one of the older women. "We've always done it this way and that's just fine by me."

Another woman warned, "If women start doing these things, the men won't be as active as they are now, and we're glad to have the men doing *something*."

The twenty-six-year-old curate who presided over the meeting said, "The church is like the family; the father always sits at the head of the table and carves the roast."

"And the mother carves the roast when the father is away," Pauli countered.

"You make a good point, Miss Murray," the young curate admitted.

"It would be nice to have a woman be the lay reader occasionally," Renee suggested in her tactful way.

Renee convinced the Reverend Allen to initiate the practice of inviting women to read the lesson from the Bible. He then also invited men to participate in traditionally female activities, such as the Altar Guild. The congregation eventually voted to elect women to vestry positions and Renee Barlow was the first woman in the history of the parish elected to be on the vestry.

Soon after, Renee took a job as personnel officer at the Executive Council of the Episcopal Church. A week later she was diagnosed with cancer. She was only fifty-three years old. Complications caused her to be in the hospital for three months and Pauli stayed by her side until she was in remission.

After tackling women's issues, Pauli began teaching law at Brandeis University in Waltham, Massachusetts, in the fall of 1968 when the Black Power movement was flexing its muscles. Pauli would be faced with confronting new ways of looking at the civil rights movement. She was now almost sixty years old, and approaches to Black empowerment were changing quickly. She had a difficult time adjusting to using the word "Black" instead of "Negro." She remembered how many years it took for W.E.B. Du Bois to successfully petition the *New York Times* to capitalize the word "Negro." Pauli told her students, "I'll try to use the term 'Black' at least *half* the time in my lectures." As a woman who had always fought for integration, considering that she herself was a product of Black, White, and Native American ancestry, she had trouble accepting the idea of Black separatism.

During this time of upheaval, Pauli was grateful for visits from Renee, though she wished for more.

"You help me heal from my loneliness," she told Renee as they walked along the Charles River with Pauli's new black Labrador retriever, Ray. "Our times together are so few and there are such long spaces in between."

Returning to New York in the summer, Pauli was happy to resume her familiar ritual of going with Renee to St. Mark's on Sundays. But the Black Power movement followed them there. James Foreman, a former member of the Student Nonviolent Coordinating Committee, known as SNCC, had written a *Black Manifesto* calling for reparations from "racist churches and synagogues" and demanding millions of dollars, which, if not granted, would be taken by force through disruptions, demonstrations, and the seizure of church buildings if necessary. He vowed to present this manifesto at various houses of worship. One such group interrupted the service at St. Mark's.

They marched down the aisle, proudly wearing colorful African dashikis, their vibrant Afro hairstyles sparkling in the reflected light of the church windows. They stood in front of the pulpit with fists raised and started with the demand for a Caucus of Black Communicants that would address Black cultural history and programs fostering Black revolution.

St. Mark's was the second oldest church in New York, and was known for its early support of dangerous civil rights actions in the

South. The Reverend Michael Allen had himself been arrested during a protest in Baltimore. Pauli knew she did not belong to a conservative church, but she was incensed by the audacity of these young people. She recalled her frustration when students at Brandeis had occupied one of the school buildings in January. Pauli wrote the reverend an angry letter, calling some of the manifesto's language a "hodge-podge of revolutionary quasi-Marxist language." She urged the church not to form a Black caucus, saying that it amounted to reverse racism and fostered separatism. At the end she asked the tantalizing question, "If the caucus's aim is to promote inclusiveness, why not include all who have been excluded from full participation in the church, namely women!"

The Reverend Allen spoke to the whole congregation in response. "How can you not see that we are a divided church? We have two congregations within these walls engaging in two different services, one White and one Black. Are we a cozy and sleepy church which, in its self-righteousness, knows it has fought the good fight (at least yesterday's fights if not today's) and now wishes to have nothing to do with the present Black battle for freedom? Are we a church who welcomes a few token Blacks to keep us from being criticized by men of goodwill? Or should we learn to live together?"

The reverend paused, bringing his gaze to each White face in the pews. "One thing is clear. The present situation of Black powerlessness has to change at St. Mark's. And elsewhere as well. For isn't that the problem of the nation?"

It was now five years since Renee's cancer had gone into remission, but she was sleeping a lot and having trouble typing. She called Pauli and said, "I've been trying to reach you but I keep dialing the wrong numbers. They've told me I have a brain tumor."

"No—" said Pauli, sitting down to take in the news. "Tell me it isn't true."

"It is, Pauli," Renee said bravely. "I've had a good life, sweetie. I don't know whether I've got what it takes to fight this thing again."

"Nonsense," Pauli replied. "If we have to go down, we'll go down fighting. I don't think God intended human beings to respond to their fate until they make every effort, but that when they have done their best, they could leave the outcome to God."

Renee entered the hospital and her condition worsened. Pauli came down to New York from Boston to stay in an apartment across the street from the hospital with Renee's sister. Pauli sat by Renee's bed, squeezing her hand and trying to hold back tears.

"Renee, we are two independent spirits who always come together in a crisis. What will happen to us?" Then Pauli rushed out of the room and down the hall to a linen closet where she wept uncontrollably before she could pull herself back together and return to the bedside of her companion of more than seventeen years.

Sometimes Pauli's heart filled with calmness and she could say, "Lord, thy will be done." Other times, she was consumed with disbelief and anger. "Lord, it isn't fair. She's only fifty-nine years old!"

On one of her visits, Pauli spoke to Renee's doctor in the hallway. "I've always been terrified of death. I never went to funerals unless I absolutely had to. I ask myself, is death the grim reaper that haunted my childhood? Or is death just a friend waiting outside the door until we are ready to go?"

The doctor answered, "I find it comforting that there is always peace on the faces of people who have died, even those who died a violent death. In the process of dying, a person may swing back and forth between two states of being, not quite out of the world and not quite in the next."

"Perhaps, we who love the person most hold them back in this process," Pauli admitted.

"Each person has a lifeline, Miss Murray. They may cling to that lifeline indefinitely. You may be that lifeline for Renee."

Pauli went back to Renee's room. The nurse had gone out and they were alone. Pauli watched in pain as her lover tossed in her bed and made small moans as she tried to keep hold of her failing breath.

Pauli whispered, "Please, God, take her. I can't bear to see her suffer this way." She opened her Bible and read aloud the 23rd Psalm. When she finished, she kissed her dying friend on the cheek and murmured quietly, "Rest."

That night Pauli returned to her temporary apartment across the street and sat by the window simply waiting while time ticked away. She clasped her hands together and bowed her head. In the stillness she sensed that she was finally able to let Renee go in peace. At 10 a.m. the next morning, Renee passed on into the next world.

When she received word of Renee's death, Pauli opened all the windows of the apartment and let

Irene Barlow, 1914-1973.

in the cold, wintry air. She played Renee's favorite piece of music, Schumann's Piano Concerto in A Minor. At Renee's funeral, she said in her eulogy, "Renee is now making joyful noises to the Lord and delighting those in heaven with her marvelous wit."

Pauli took care of all the details of the service at Calvary Episcopal Church where Eleanor Roosevelt had been christened. Afterward, the reverend complimented her on the fine service. "You may not have realized it," he said, "but you have been acting as an enabler, a function of a deacon in our church. You and your friend Renee were engaged in a Christian ministry. Now that she is gone, you can carry it on for both." He looked at her quietly. "Have you thought about ordination to the position of deacon?"

"But women aren't allowed," Pauli objected.

The reverend only smiled. "One never knows what the Lord has in mind for us."

Pauli contemplated Renee's death and her own spiritual path as she drove back to Boston that afternoon. As she drove north, a many-hued sunset spread across the sky. Clouds of gold transformed into turquoise and pink, and finally a peaceful lavender descended over the sky as the sun receded beyond the horizon. She saw the exquisite beauty of the sunset as a testament to the spirit of her soulmate.

Renee's death made a profound impression upon Pauli. She realized she had read the liturgy at the bedside of two devout Christians when they were in their final hours—her beloved aunt, whom she called "Mother," and her most loyal friend who was also her lover. She kept going back to the words of the priest who had suggested she become ordained, even though the ordination of women was not yet allowed in the Episcopal church.

She was now sixty-three years old with a tenured position as a law professor at Brandeis University. But, true to her questing spirit, she gave it all up and moved to New York to enter the General Theological Seminary as a one-year special student preparing for holy orders. She was accepted by a bishop who had lectured the House of Bishops that Christ in the Second Coming might be a person of a different sex or race than Jesus. But the General Episcopal Convention had just met and voted down the approval for ordaining women. The next convention was another three years away.

Pauli applied for the three-year Master of Divinity program in the hope that when she finished, the convention would finally approve women's ordination.

She wrote her niece Bonnie, with whom she continued a long correspondence:

The program is the most rigorous of all my academic training. Not only is there a great deal to learn, one's personality is under the continuous scrutiny of instructors and schoolmates, as well as under constant self-examination. In addition to the daily devotions and corporate worship, seminarians have to satisfy the various layers of the church hierarchy that they are not only academically competent but also that the spiritual formation essential to a priestly calling is plainly evident in their bearing.

In her final year, Pauli applied to the Virginia Theological Seminary so she could do her internship at Saint Philip's Chapel in Aquasco, Maryland, Prince George's County.

Again, she wrote to Bonnie:

> It is the same little mission church in which your great-uncle, Reverend Small, served as vicar fifty years ago. Some of the infants he baptized then are now grandparents and leaders of the congregation. The oldest communicant, a man named Peter Brooks, remembered me as a little girl. Members of Saint Philip's have never had a seminarian serve their church before, and they were so pleased that I cared enough to remember and come back to this small rural congregation, they adopted me with pride and affection. Knowing that Aunt Pauline, Aunt Sallie, and Grandmother Cornelia all worshiped there many years before links me with my past and gives continuity to my spiritual pilgrimage.

Pauli had too much anxiety to attend the General Convention in Minneapolis, where the fate of women in the church would be decided. She didn't think she could overcome another barrier put up to prevent her from fulfilling her purpose in life. With her only companion, her black Labrador, Ray, Pauli stayed at home and quietly prayed for the best outcome.

She received a telephone call from an unlikely source.

"Is this Miss Pauli Murray?" the voice on the other end of the line asked.

"Yes, it is," said Pauli.

"I just had to contact you, Miss Murray. Oh, excuse me, I forgot to introduce myself in my excitement. I am calling from the General Convention in Minneapolis. I am Reverend Peter James Lee, rector of the Chapel of the Cross in Chapel Hill, North Carolina. You know the church, of course?"

"I do, indeed. My grandmother, Cornelia Smith, was baptized there as a child."

"Yes, I read about your family's story in your wonderful book, *Proud Shoes*. But before I get to that, have you heard the decision?"

"No, my goodness, no. I haven't heard yet."

"Well, then, let me have the special honor of being the first to tell you the great Good News! The Convention has voted to allow the ordination of women!"

Pauli was speechless for a moment. "Oh, my goodness, the Lord be praised," she quoted Aunt Pauline. "Reverend Lee, I am going to have to sit down for a moment."

Pauli sat down on the couch as Ray got up to sit beside her. She held the phone in one hand and stroked Ray's head with the other.

"Oh, dear, this is an important moment for you," said the reverend. "I should contact you another time. But I was so excited, I wanted to call you right away before anyone else got to you."

"I'm sorry, I don't understand."

"I want to invite you to celebrate your first Holy Eucharist as a priest at the Chapel of the Cross here in Durham."

"You or I must be dreaming," Pauli murmured incredulously.

"On the contrary. I can think of no more appropriate symbol of what has happened here today than having you preside at the altar in the same chapel building where your grandmother Cornelia was baptized in 1854."

"I don't know what to say," Pauli stammered.

"Don't worry," answered Reverend Lee cheerfully. "I'll send you the details in a letter soon. But you will say yes, won't you?"

"Yes, yes, of course! I believe that would be the most right and fitting thing to do, Reverend Lee. Thank you for the invitation."

As soon as she put down the receiver, the telephone rang again. It was the Right Reverend Morris F. Arnold, who had ordained her as a deacon the previous June.

"I was thinking about you during the voting and I want to move right along to prepare for your ordination to the priesthood. Instead of coming all the way up to Boston to your own diocese for the ordination, I would like to arrange for you to be ordained at the National Cathedral in Washington, DC. The Right Reverend William F. Creighton will be presiding."

"Bishop Creighton, who has refused to ordain anyone—male or female, until the convention passes on this issue?" said Pauli. "I would be so proud to be inducted in his presence."

The time came on a gray day in Washington, DC, when Pauli Murray was ordained with three young men and two older women who had become priests in alternative ceremonies. They made their way in the procession, following the long line of clergy in their fine clerical gowns. Six prayer desks were set in a semicircle around the bishops and other clergy. The six ordinants moved to stand behind them.

Finally, it was Pauli's turn to be consecrated. She stood in front of Bishop Creighton so that he could place his hands on her forehead in blessing. A quiet hush filled the great hall. As he touched her forehead, the clouds outside separated and sent bands of light through the stained-glass windows in all colors of the rainbow, causing the congregation to gasp in wonder. As soon as he uttered the words, "The Peace of the Lord be always with you," an outburst of pure joy and affirmation thundered through the consecrated halls of the National Cathedral.

Chapter 21

Chapel Hill

The Reverend Pauli Murray had one more important journey to make—to return to her home parish in Chapel Hill, North Carolina, to the church where her grandmother, born a slave, had been baptized.

Charles Kuralt, the CBS News journalist who traveled around the county doing human interest stories for his Sunday morning show, *On the Road with Charles Kuralt*, wanted to be there when this independent, accomplished woman celebrated her first Eucharist. He had a special interest in Reverend Murray's story, since he was from North Carolina and a graduate of the University of North Carolina, which was first built on land bequeathed by her family's Smith ancestors.

On Sunday, February 13, 1977, Kuralt joined the Reverend on her trip home. They first ventured to her grandparent's house at the bottom of the cemetery. It was well kept and freshly painted, though no longer in the family. With her dog Ray, Pauli climbed the worn steps up to the front porch where she had read the newspaper to Grandfather Fitzgerald after his eyesight had failed. And where her grandmother Cornelia had shouted to the neighbors to keep clear of the field in front of her property.

Pauli always had a favorite Labrador as her companion.

Kuralt spoke with a genteel Southern drawl. "Do you feel reconciled with your own past, all the different elements of it, Reverend Murray? You have all these cross-currents of violence and pain that meet—in you."

Pauli looked at the White folks' gravestones that had always frightened her as a child, and let out a great laugh. "Yes, I know. I've lived with those cross-currents for sixty-six years. It's like riding wild horses." She turned to Kuralt and spoke seriously. "I am tempestuous, volatile. I have a tremendous amount of nervous energy. My friends say I can wear out six people. I have an Irish African temper—of which there is no worse," she laughed.

Pauli turned and came down the porch steps, sitting on the middle step, stroking Ray's ears before she continued. "I am sensitive, aggressive, shy. I am all of these warring personalities, trying to stay in one integrated body, mind, and spirit." She looked up with an impish smile on her face. "And there are days when I bless my ancestors. And there are other days when I look in the mirror and I say, What hath God wrought?"

Then it was time for the service. The reverend and the journalist paused as they entered the sanctuary of the Chapel of the Cross. They looked at the book that carried the old church records of births and deaths and baptisms since the church was founded in 1848. There, in beautiful cursive letters in faded brown ink, were the words: "Five Servant Children Belonging to Miss Mary Ruffin Smith." Listed below were Cornelia Smith, age ten; her three half-sisters born of Sidney Smith's brother Frank; and her older half-brother, born of Ruben Day, her mother Harriett's husband who was run off the plantation.

As they walked into the church, they saw six hundred people, both Black and White, crowded into the chapel, which was only meant for two hundred and fifty souls. Pauli stood at the lectern, an ornate mahogany dais carved with the spreading wings of an eagle. It was inscribed on the front, "In Memory of Mary Ruffin Smith, 1888."

Pauli opened the Bible given to her grandmother Cornelia by her father, Sidney Smith. Her fingers traveled to the pages marked by the purple ribbon that had graced the flowers Mrs. Roosevelt had given her upon her graduation from Howard. She read aloud, "The holy gospel of the Lord Jesus Christ according to Luke: And as ye would that men should do to you, do ye also to them likewise."

The Reverend Peter James Lee delivered a sermon dedicated to Dr. Reverend Pauli Murray.

Pauli Murray in Eucharistic vestments at lectern.

Pauli took her time administering the Eucharist, cherishing her individual greeting with each parishioner as she engaged in that sacred rite. At the end of the service, she joyously proclaimed, "The peace of the Lord always be with you."

Walking outside after the service, Pauli commented to Kuralt, "What I was trying to communicate as I administered the bread was a lovingness for each individual who received the bread, and I went very slowly. I didn't care how long it took."

Pauli mused, "My great-grandmother, Sarah Ann, a White woman from Delaware, always said, 'We're all just betwixt and between.' I believe in reconciling the descendants of all the slaves and all the slave owners of the South. And by now, the genes have recirculated so that, I suspect, if you put all of the people of the United States end to end, according to their true blood line, we'd all be in one long line, all of us. That's the fascinating thing about the South. Black, White, and Red are all related by blood and by culture, and by history and by common suffering."

Pauli spread her hands out wide in a gesture of encircling, then clasped them beneath her chin. "Look, let's level with one another; let's admit we are related and let's get on with the business of healing these wounds. We're not going to heal them unless we face the truth."

For the next eight years Pauli never rested, always seeking ways to find reconciliation and healing for all the souls to whom she ministered in so many different ways. She never officiated in her own church, but she was in great demand as a preacher in churches in Washington, DC, and Pittsburgh, as well as her home parish in Baltimore.

Writer, activist, lawyer, priest; African, Irish, Cherokee. Harboring a masculine sensibility in a woman's body, Pauli's warring selves had at last found a meaningful home in her body, mind, and spirit. She was seventy-five years old and had no intention of retiring when her frail body gave out on July 1, 1985, after a life fully lived in spite of the numerous obstacles she had to overcome. By taking part in sit-ins ten years before the civil rights movement, introducing the argument that separate institutions were inherently unequal before the Brown v. Board of Education decision enshrined that idea into law, and insisting that discrimination by gender was similar to racial discrimination, Pauli Murray influenced the cause of human rights for all people, leaving behind a lasting legacy.

Acknowledgments

I am grateful to the first readers of my manuscript, Andrea Jepson, Mary Sherman Willis, and Marita Golden, who gave me valuable advice. I give special thanks to my husband Peter Kuznick for helping me find Rootstock Publishing and for his unwavering support throughout this project. Simha Stubblefield provided an insightful reading of the final manuscript.

About the Author

Simki Kuznick grew up in the Bay Area before she moved to Washington, DC, where she had a long career as an editor for the US Government. Her writing focuses on what people with multicultural and multiracial heritage can bring to our understanding of what it is to be American. She edited a monthly newspaper, *Poetry San Francisco*, and was a founding member of Interracial Pride in Berkeley, California, while raising two daughters with her first husband who is from Eritrea. She completed her MFA in Creative Writing at American University in 2010. Her poetry explores the interactions between cultures in Africa, Asia, and Eastern Europe. She and her husband, Peter Kuznick, co-author of *The Untold History of the United States* with Oliver Stone, live in Bethesda, Maryland, along with their numerous reptiles and amphibians.

Also Available from Rootstock Publishing:

The Atomic Bomb on My Back by Taniguchi Sumiteru

Pauli Murray's Revolutionary Life by Simki Kuznick

Blue Desert by Celia Jeffries

China in Another Time: A Personal Story by Claire Malcolm Lintilhac

Collecting Courage: Anti-Black Racism in the Charitable Sector
Edited by Nneka Allen, Camila Vital Nunes Pereira, & Nicole Salmon

An Everyday Cult by Gerette Buglion

Fly with A Murder of Crows: A Memoir by Tuvia Feldman

Horodno Burning: A Novel by Michael Freed-Thall

I Could Hardly Keep from Laughing by Don Hooper & Bill Mares

The Inland Sea: A Mystery by Sam Clark

Intent to Commit by Bernie Lambek

Junkyard at No Town by J.C. Myers

The Language of Liberty: A Citizen's Vocabulary by Edwin C. Hagenstein

A Lawyer's Life to Live by Kimberly B. Cheney

Lifting Stones: Poems by Doug Stanfield

The Lost Grip: Poems by Eva Zimet

Lucy Dancer Story and Illustrations by Eva Zimet

Nobody Hitchhikes Anymore by Ed Griffin-Nolan

Preaching Happiness: Creating a Just and Joyful World by Ginny Sassaman

Red Scare in the Green Mountains: Vermont in the McCarthy Era 1946-1960
by Rick Winston

Safe as Lightning: Poems by Scudder H. Parker

Street of Storytellers by Doug Wilhelm

Tales of Bialystok: A Jewish Journey from Czarist Russia to America
by Charles Zachariah Goldberg

To the Man in the Red Suit: Poems by Christina Fulton

Uncivil Liberties: A Novel by Bernie Lambek

Venice Beach: A Novel by William Mark Habeeb

The Violin Family by Melissa Perley; Illustrated by Fiona Lee Maclean

Walking Home: Trail Stories by Celia Ryker

Wave of the Day: Collected Poems by Mary Elizabeth Winn

Whole Worlds Could Pass Away: Collected Stories by Rickey Gard Diamond

You Have a Hammer: Building Grant Proposals for Social Change by Barbara Floersch

CPSIA information can be obtained
at www.ICGtesting.com
Printed in the USA
LVHW111529110422
715890LV00002B/41